Also by Richard Roeper

He Rents, She Rents (with Laurie Viera)

Urban Legends

Hollywood Urban Legends

*10 Sure Signs a Movie Character Is Doomed
& Other Surprising Movie Lists*

HOLLYWOOD AT ITS WORST

Richard Roeper

HYPERION NEW YORK

For my mother:

So wonderful she's like something out of a movie.

A few passages in this book were previously published in the *Chicago Sun-Times* in a slightly different form.

Library of Congress Cataloging-in-Publication Data

Roeper, Richard, 1959–
    Schlock value : Hollywood at its worst / Richard Roeper.—1st. ed.
        p. cm.
    ISBN: 1-4013-0769-8
    1. Motion pictures—United States—Anecdotes. I. Title.

    PN1993.5.U6R596 2004
    791.43'0973—dc22

                                        2004052372

Hyperion books are available for special promotions and premiums. For details contact Michael Rentas, Manager, Inventory and Premium Sales, Hyperion, 77 West 66th Street, 11th floor, New York, New York, 10023-6298, or call 212-456-0133.

FIRST EDITION

10 9 8 7 6 5 4 3 2 1

Acknowledgments

Thanks to Robert and Margaret Roeper; Lynn and Nick Zona; Bob and Colleen Roeper; Laura Roeper; Sam Saunders; Laura LeQuesne; John LeQuesne; Emily Roeper; Caroline Roeper; Bobby Roeper.

Also: Bill Adee, Grace Adee, Joe Ahern, Leslie Baldacci, John Barron, Anna Butler, Michael Cavoto, Michelle Carney, Jennifer Ciminillo, Michael Cooke, John Cruickshank, Darcie Divita, Don Dupree, Roger Ebert, Laura Emerick, Robert Feder, Carol Fowler, Rebekah Furgeson, Wendy George, Drew Hayes, Holly Herckis, Susanna Homan, Jon Kaplan, Mary Kellogg, David Kodeski, Rick Kogan, Blagodat Kondeva, Janet LaMonica, Todd Musburger, David Plummer, Phil and Jennie and Zachary Rosenthal, Nancy Stanley, Neil Steinberg, Will Taylor, Christy Van House, Jenniffer Weigel and the Wisers: Paige, Jim and Audrey.

Special thanks to my Not-At-All-Big-Not-At-All-Fat-But-Very-Greek assistant Lia Papadopoulos.

Deepest thanks to my agent, Sheree Bykofsky, who always believes in me.

Sincere thanks to everyone at Hyperion, notably my editor, Ben Loehnen. You're the best.

Introduction

Every movie fan knows these truths to be self-evident:

Chris Rock and Vin Diesel are movie stars. The most successful movie of all time is *Titanic*. Every critic in the nation panned *Gigli*. Russell Crowe and Salma Hayek have never made a film together. Winning a Golden Globe is the next best thing to taking home an Academy Award. *Pretty Woman* made far more money than *The Graduate*. Accepting Best Actor honors for *Philadelphia*, Tom Hanks made one of the greatest Oscar speeches of all time.

And the human head weights eight pounds.

Reasonable statements—except they're not based in truth. Yes, Chris Rock and Vin Diesel are famous and they get paid a lot of money to headline films, but neither has turned in a single performance worthy of the "movie star" tag. Not one.

Russell Crowe and Salma Hayek actually did make a movie together. It's just that nobody saw it. As for the respective box office grosses for *Titanic*, *Pretty Woman* and *The Graduate*, the rankings depend on whether we're going to adjust the figures for inflation. And if we're not, then we're just perpetuating lazy myths.

What about *Gigli*? Was it not raw meat for barking critics? Absolutely! Yet a few critics actually praised the film, and as far as we know none was on crack at the time.

The Golden Globes? A golden crock.

Tom Hanks' heartfelt and emotional acceptance speech at the Oscars? It might have brought you to tears, but study the transcript and you'll realize the man was making little sense. Mostly, he was babbling.

And the human head does *not* weigh eight pounds, despite what the kid in *Jerry Maguire* would have you believe. Not even if we adjust it for inflation.

Everyone loves to talk about the movies. Every day for the last four-plus years, somebody has approached me to strike up a film-related conversation. I'll be having dinner, and someone will interrupt and say, "I don't mean to interrupt, but we're going to see *Alien vs. Predator* tonight, did you like it?" I'll be getting a chest X-ray, and a technician will say, "Take a deep breath and hold it—and when I get back I want to ask you about the Sundance Film Festival!" I'll be waiting for my ridiculously complicated coffee drink and another customer will tap me on the shoulder and say, "What were you thinking when you recommended *Taking Lives*?"

And, I swear to God this is true, at least once a month someone will ask the golden question: "Do you have to see all those movies before you review them?"

What a novel approach. *See* the movies *before* we review them! That's going to make it so much easier than giving an opinion based on the coming attractions.

But I wouldn't trade those moments for anything, because I'm seeing movies for a living, and yes, it's as much fun as it sounds.

Most of the time.

You might think a book about movies titled *Schlock Value* would be a ripping indictment of the art and the industry— and I do take my shots at the actors and the directors and the trends and the clichés that deserve it—but this book is for movie fans, written by a movie fan. If I hated movies, if I were some anonymous, newsgroup-dwelling snob who believed the last quality film came out in 1974, what would be the point in working as a film critic? Prolonged masochism? Why write (or read) a book that exposes some of the sillier and darker aspects of the industry if you don't care about movies in the first place? It's our obsession for movies that creates the interest in some of the schlockier things about the business, the artists and, yes, the critics.

Not that *Schlock Value* is all negative. When I take you behind the scenes on *Ebert & Roeper*, or when I list movies that went straight to video or cable because they were abandoned by the studios, or when I list the obscene prices of the snack foods at a typical concession stand, I'm doing it all with a big fat smile.

Because when you love something the way I love movies, you delight in the flaws almost as much as you appreciate the positives.

chapter 1

Attack of the Hacks

If the entire world lined up according to comedic talent, we could be certain of two things:

> **1.** Carrot Top, Rob Schneider, Pauly Shore and Tom Green would be bonding in the far reaches of our 6.3 billion-person queue, behind such prominent humorists as Dick Cheney, your neighborhood butcher and either Olsen twin.

> **2.** Chris Rock would be at the very front of that humor line—maybe even leading the parade.

Rock just might be the funniest person on the planet. As a stand-up comedian, he has harnessed the raw brilliance that was evident when he was a teenager and has become an ice-cool master of the craft—a worthy successor to Bill Cosby, George Carlin, Richard Pryor, Steve Martin and Eddie Murphy, perhaps the five best pure stand-ups of the last half-century. Rock's scathing insights on race are brave and funny and painfully true, his social observations are poignant and bullshit-free, and his views on romance and relationships are priceless. (He's also a gutsy performer—a rare famous person who's willing to offend his fellow residents of Celebrity Nation in pursuit of the memorable laugh. At the 2003 MTV Video Music Awards, Rock dared the audience to laugh with one-liners such as, "Having Paula Abdul judge a singing contest is like having Christopher Reeve judging a dance contest!") Rock is also an edgy and self-effacing ad-lib artist, as evidenced by his HBO series and specials, his appearances on *The Tonight Show with Jay Leno* and *Late Show with David Letterman*, his awards show work on MTV and his guest stints on Howard Stern's radio show, a forum where many a lesser talent has floundered and flopped like Nemo on a cold floor.

But what about the comic as an actor? Though the very young Chris Rock was never fully utilized on *Saturday Night Live*, he did flash some potential in a few skits, and that promise looked even brighter after Rock's critically acclaimed, straight-dramatic portrayal of a crack addict who can't stay clean in the under-appreciated *New Jack City* (1991). It was a juicy, nasty little part, and he nailed it.

All the pieces were in place for Rock to become a force in feature films. Gifted with enormous talent, loads of street smarts and show-biz savvy, he seemed like the perfect candidate for major movie stardom.

Until he actually started making movies, one after another, and they sucked, one after another.

Even as his stand-up career soared, Chris Rock the thespian spent much of the 1990s doing forgettable supporting work in such mediocre, middle-of-the-road dreck as *Panther*, *The Immortals*, *Sgt. Bilko*, *Beverly Hills Ninja*, *Lethal Weapon 4* and *Doctor Doolittle*. (He also did *Dogma*, Kevin Smith's bold and interesting religious satire, in which Rock appeared nude and facedown on a highway, like skinny roadkill.) Examine that roster again, and imagine having to sit through all of those films in a home viewing marathon. The mere thought of it brings you to the edge of tears, doesn't it? We're talking about the kind of films that are mentioned prominently on Comedy Central roasts—and conveniently ignored during career tributes.

Still, you can't place all the blame on Rock for these disasters, any more than you can blame the backup catcher for the 2003 Detroit Tigers for a 43–119 season. Rock was just a supporting player—a bench guy who did what he could with limited playing time. It ain't Chris Rock's fault that *Lethal Weapon 4* is toothless junk.

So what happened when Rock was given the opportunity to be the featured attraction and in some cases a behind-the-scenes force? The movies actually got worse. A lot worse. From *Down to Earth*, an idiotic, cheesy and flat-out unfunny rip-off of *Heaven Can Wait*, to *Bad Company*, an idiotic, cheesy and flat-out unfunny rip-off of *48 HRS.*, to *Head of State* (which Rock also wrote, produced and directed), an idiotic, cheesy and flat-out unfunny rip-off of *Dave*, Rock starred in a succession of disappointing and curiously safe vehicles that are more depressing than the latter part of Gene Wilder's film career. (I won't even mention the execrable *Pootie Tang* other than to say that if you're ever tempted to rent, watch or own *Pootie Tang*, lock yourself in a room until that temptation goes away.)

How did this happen? How did someone as smart and talented as Chris Rock take a string of supporting parts that might easily have gone to a Gilbert Gottfried or even a (shudder) Bobcat Goldthwait in an even crueler movie world? And once Rock was given the chance to do above-the-title roles, was he offered nothing better than, for example, the retread buddy-movie *Bad Company*? Was there nobody in Rock's life who could have told him that his own scripts for *Down to Earth* and *Head of State* were clunkers—that the roles he wrote for himself were one-dimensional clichés, far beneath his talents as a comedic actor?

Apparently not.

Movies are hard. Even if you've been magic-wanded with heavy doses of talent, charisma and great good fortune, even if you have a great work ethic and a keen sense of the business and you've managed to avoid career death by sex, drugs, booze, money, stupidity or your own ego—even if you're Jack Nicholson, for Chrissake—you're not going to have a 1.000 career batting average. Nobody bats 1.000. Meryl Streep is a genius, and she's savvy, and she's picky. Throughout her career, Streep has made wise choices, and she's had an amazing run filled with memorable performances in classy fare. Yet her filmography includes *Plenty*, *Falling in Love*, *She-Devil* and *Before and After*. Watch those duds back-to-back-to-back-to-back, and you've just had an eight-hour preview of life in purgatory.

Overall, though, Streep is a first-ballot Hall of Famer who's batting about .750 for her career, meaning that about three of every four films in which she appears are worth your time and money. (We're talking about the quality of the films, not necessarily the box-office results—though if a film grosses a couple hundred mil, I'd be inclined to include it in the "lucky hit" category and give the actor credit for it as a quality at-bat. A commercial hit can provide the fuel to rocket an actor through a few major studio flops and also give her the security to try one or two smaller films.) Other stars hitting in the general stratosphere of 75 percent include the aforementioned Mr. Nicholson, Tom Hanks, Al Pacino, Robert De Niro, Dustin Hoffman, Robert Redford, Paul Newman, Jane Fonda, Denzel Washington and Julianne Moore, along with such young stars as Tobey Maguire and Matt Damon. Dozens of other actors, from Julia Roberts to Meg Ryan, Gwyneth Paltrow, Kirsten Dunst, Brittany Murphy and Jake Gyllenhaal, have a

success rate of about 50 percent. They're .500 hitters—
equally as likely to appear in a good film as a bad one.

Chris Rock? He's hitting about .100.

They get star billing in one movie after another. They're paid
hundreds of thousands of dollars, or in some cases millions
of dollars, to act in major studio films. They walk red carpets
and they joke it up with Jay and Dave and Conan, they're in
regular rotation on the E! video jukebox, and they're often
asked for their autographs by adoring fans. Magazines such
as Us, People and In Touch take photos of them when they're
having lunch at the Ivy or getting coffee at Starbucks.

Only one hitch: Their films are consistently, inevitably, ir-
refutably crappy. Following we have some of the less successful stars of the last fifteen years, with the focus primarily on
the young or at least youngish actors who are still getting offered major roles in mainstream fare. (What's the point of
listing the numerous flops starring a Sylvester Stallone or a
Linda Fiorentino when they're no longer appearing in big
studio releases on a regular basis?) I've listed some of their
more prominent hits and misses, but the "career batting average" is for the entire body of work—and the batting average
is the percentage of quality films as determined by, well, me.

MADONNA

Work of value: *Evita* (1996), and supporting work in *A League of Their Own* (1992), *Dick Tracy* (1990), *Desperately Seeking Susan* (1985)*

Cinematic crimes: *Swept Away* (2002), *The Next Best Thing* (2001), *Body of Evidence* (1993), *Who's That Girl?* (1987), *Shanghai Surprise* (1986)

(*Madonna was the title character in *Susan*, but Rosanna Arquette owned the movie.)

Career batting average: 28 percent

FREDDIE PRINZE JR.

Work of value: *The House of Yes* (1997)

Cinematic crimes: *Scooby-Doo 2: Monsters Unleashed* (2004), *Scooby-Doo* (2002), *Summer Catch* (2001), *Boys and Girls* (2000), *I Still Know What You Did Last Summer* (1998)

Career batting average: 14 percent

CHRIS KATTAN

Work of value: None to date.

Cinematic crimes: *Corky Romano* (2001), *MonkeyBone* (2001), *A Night at the Roxbury* (1998)

Career batting average: 0 percent

DAVID SPADE

Work of value: *Tommy Boy* (1995)

Cinematic crimes: *Dickie Roberts: Former Child Star*

(2003), *Joe Dirt* (2001), *Lost & Found* (1999), *Coneheads* (1993)

Career batting average: 17 percent

SANDRA BULLOCK

Work of value: *A Time to Kill* (1996), *Speed* (1994)

Cinematic crimes: *Divine Secrets of the Ya-Ya Sisterhood* (2002), *Two Weeks Notice* (2002), *Miss Congeniality* (2000), *Speed 2: Cruise Control* (1997), *Two If by Sea* (1996)

Career batting average: 20 percent

DAVID DUCHOVNY

Work of value: *Kalifornia* (1993)

Cinematic crimes: *Full Frontal* (2002), *Evolution* (2001), *Return to Me* (2000), *Playing God* (1997)

Career batting average: 20 percent

DREW BARRYMORE

Work of value: *Confessions of a Dangerous Mind* (2002), *E.T. The Extra-Terrestrial* (1982)

Cinematic crimes: *50 First Dates* (2004), *Duplex* (2003), *Charlie's Angels: Full Throttle* (2003), *Freddy Got Fingered* (2001), *Never Been Kissed* (1999), *Batman Forever* (1995), *Bad Girls* (1994), *Poison Ivy* (1992)

Career batting average: 19 percent

JOSH HARTNETT

Work of value: *The Virgin Suicides* (2000); *Black Hawk Down* (2001)

Cinematic crimes: *40 Days and 40 Nights* (2002), *Pearl Harbor* (2001), *Blow Dry* (2001)

Career batting average: 30 percent

TARA REID

Work of value: *American Pie* (1999), tiny role in *The Big Lebowski* (1998)

Cinematic crimes: *National Lampoon's Van Wilder* (2002), *Body Shots* (1999), *Urban Legend* (1998)

Career batting average: 28 percent

MARTIN LAWRENCE

Work of value: *Bad Boys* (1995)

Cinematic crimes: *Bad Boys II* (2003), *Black Knight* (2001), *What's the Worst That Could Happen?* (2001), *Big Momma's House* (2000), *Life* (1999)

Career batting average: 12 percent

I have a light resentment for the Tara Reids and the Martin Lawrences and the David Spades for stealing all those hours of viewing time from me—hours that could have been spent on more productive activities, such as systematically pounding my head against a hard surface—but actors are often hired hands, serving at the pleasure of the filmmaker, and the only films they can appear in are the films that come their way. (It's not as if Tara Reid is getting offers to do *Lost in Translation* or even *Starsky & Hutch*.) The director is the primary author of the movie, and the argument can be made that a Michael Bay is a dozen times more poisonous than a Josh Hartnett. The amiable Hartnett is young and good-looking and earnest, and he's done enough competent work that one might reasonably believe he can achieve an Alec Baldwin–level career some day, but Bay's five major films tell us that he's not the least bit interested in doing anything other than spending prodigious amounts of cash in order to blow things up and set records for the most quick cuts in an action movie. Bay's *Bad Boys II* might well be the ugliest, meanest and most cynical movie of the last ten years. It is truly soulless.

Ninety-nine percent of moviegoers don't know the identities of the directors who inflict their mediocrity on us. They don't connect the dots from *Soul Man* to *Halloween H20* to *The Texas Rangers*. They don't realize that the same man is responsible for all three films. Only great directors become famous. Ford, Hitchcock, Spielberg, Scorsese, Coppola—you know them because they have created lasting art, multiple times. You will not recognize the names of most of the directors on this list, but, sadly, you will be familiar with their work. I think you'll agree with me that collectively they have turned out enough junk to fill the remainder bin near the checkout counter at the drugstore. ("Honey, should we buy this movie for a buck ninety-eight? It's got that Andrew Dice Clay guy, remember him? Ah screw it, I'll get a couple of Butterfingers instead . . .") Some of these filmmakers, like Michael Lehmann, made impressive directorial debuts, but then inexplicably fell into the abyss of hackwork. (One imagines a veteran grip on the set of *My Giant* or *40 Days and 40 Nights* telling an incredulous young second assistant director that Lehmann once brushed greatness with *Heathers*.) Others started out on a hot streak and are undeniably talented. They should always be credited and thanked for their early work—but they should also be chided for the assembly-line muck they've been turning out for the last several years. With the possible exception of Michael Bay, nobody ever *intends* to make a bad film. Nevertheless, that's what these directors have done, on a regular basis.

MICHAEL BAY

Work of value: *Bad Boys* (1995)

Cinematic crimes: *Bad Boys II* (2003), *Pearl Harbor* (2001), *Armageddon* (1998), *The Rock* (1996)

Career batting average: 20 percent

RENNY HARLIN

Work of value: *Die Hard 2: Die Harder* (1990)

Cinematic crimes: *Driven* (2001), *The Long Kiss Goodnight* (1996), *Cutthroat Island* (1995), *The Adventures of Ford Fairlane* (1990)

Career batting average: 18 percent

STEVE MINER

Work of value: *Forever Young* (1992)

Cinematic crimes: *The Texas Rangers* (2001), *Halloween: H2O* (1998), *My Father, the Hero* (1994), *Warlock* (1991), *Soul Man* (1986)

Career batting average: 8 percent

ROBERT ISCOVE

Work of value: None to date

Cinematic crimes: *From Justin to Kelly* (2003), *Boys and Girls* (2000), *She's All That* (1999), *Without Warning* (1994)

Career batting average: 0 percent

DONALD PETRIE

Work of value: *Mystic Pizza* (1988)

Cinematic crimes: *How to Lose a Guy in 10 Days* (2003), *Miss Congeniality* (2000), *My Favorite Martian* (1999), *Richie Rich* (1994), *Opportunity Knocks* (1990)

Career batting average: 20 percent

RAJA GOSNELL

Work of value: None to date

Cinematic crimes: *Scooby-Doo 2: Monsters Unleashed* (2004), *Scooby-Doo* (2002), *Big Momma's House* (2000), *Never Been Kissed* (1999), *Home Alone 3* (1997)

Career batting average: 0 percent

SAM WEISMAN

Work of value: None to date

Cinematic crimes: *What's the Worst That Could Happen?* (2001), *The Out-of-Towners* (1999), *George of the Jungle* (1997)

Career batting average: 0 percent

BRIAN LEVANT

Work of value: The first *Beethoven* (1992) was kinda cute.

Cinematic crimes: *The Flintstones in Viva Rock Vegas* (2000), *Jingle All the Way* (1996), *Problem Child 2* (1991)

Career batting average: 17 percent

MICHAEL LEHMANN

Work of value: *Heathers* (1989)

Cinematic crimes: *40 Days and 40 Nights* (2002), *My Giant* (1998), *Hudson Hawk* (1991)

Career batting average: 29 percent

You can't be an idiot *and* a director of major studio films. You just can't. Can you? No, I'm reasonably certain about this: You can't. Before a studio will entrust you with $50 million and put you in charge of hundreds of film professionals, you must have demonstrated some measurable talent, some kind of track record, some kind of *vision*.

One would think it's a similar story with actors. If you're

starring in a motion picture, surely you've displayed some kind of talent level or photogenic magic that sets you apart from the thousands of aspiring actors who never make it to that level. You can't just be a charmless, extremely lucky dolt. Can you?

The *Scooby-Doo* movies notwithstanding, I can't in good conscience advocate actual legislation to prohibit Raja Gosnell and Freddie Prinze Jr. from teaming up on another project. All I can do is hope and pray that if they do work together again, they'll reach down into the untapped reservoirs of their respective artistic gifts and produce a minor miracle: a movie that doesn't reek.

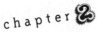

Money Changes Everything

On Monday morning, May 19, 2003, there was a giant buzz about one of the most highly anticipated sequels of all time: *The Matrix: Reloaded*. Nearly every major newspaper and newscast in the country reported on the box office performance for the film, which actually debuted in select theaters at 10 P.M. on Wednesday, May 14, a day prior to its "official" opening. You'd have been hard-pressed to find a single newspaper in the country that didn't run a story about the five-day scorecard for the film.

"*The Matrix: Reloaded* opened with an estimated four-day box-office payload of $135.8 million," reported the *Atlanta Journal-Constitution*. "That's a record for a Thursday to Sunday opening. And a record for an R-rated film."

Referencing a term made popular in the early stages of the U.S. war with Iraq, the New York *Daily News* report said, "*The Matrix: Reloaded* unleashed its own shock and awe on movie theaters this weekend. [The film had] the second most lucrative three-day weekend in movie history, trailing only *Spider-Man* . . . [that] means that one of the most expensive films in history is on its way to becoming one of the most successful."

Other newspapers, including the *Los Angeles Times*, reported the same numbers, but gave them a slightly negative spin.

"*Spider-Man's* record is safe for another day," wrote the *Times*. "*The Matrix: Reloaded* grossed an estimated $93.3 million in its first full weekend at the box office, a mammoth debut that nevertheless fell well short of the *Spider-Man* opening weekend record of $114 million."

Of course, that *Reloaded* opened late on Wednesday and ran all day on Thursday meant that many hardcore fans would have already seen it, maybe more than once, before the traditional Friday-to-Sunday weekend. Also, *Spider-Man* was rated PG-13 while *Reloaded* was an R, meaning *Spidey* had a larger audience pool in the first place. But most stories buried or ignored those salient points. Who has time for such nuances? Certainly not the readers!

The Matrix: Reloaded was also a hot topic on the morning TV shows on the first Monday after its premiere. On *The Early Show* on CBS, Julie Chen chatted up *People* magazine's Jess Cagle, who, to his credit, pointed out that the weekend tally was somewhat deflated because the movie had already been in theaters for a couple of days. *Reloaded's* $93 million opening weekend "would have been even higher had the movie not opened on a Wednesday," said Cagle.

CHEN: *"It would have been even higher?"*

CAGLE: *"It would have. A lot of people were expecting that the movie would . . . outdo* Spider-Man, *which still holds the record [for an opening] weekend gross . . . like, $115 million last year."*

CHEN: *"Wow."*

Wow indeed.

Cagle also said that the stellar performance of *Reloaded* was encouraging for Warner Brothers because "the third [*Matrix*] movie, which comes out in November, cost a lot more than that first one to make," to which Chen replied, "Oh my gosh!"

Meanwhile, on *Good Morning America*, news anchor Robin Roberts said, "It was a whopper of a weekend at the box office for *The Matrix: Reloaded*. Dare I say huge? In addition to being second to *Spider-Man* on the all-time list, the estimated $93 million take [was] a record for the debut of an R-rated movie. *Daddy Day Care* remains in second place. And *X2: X-Men United* in third."

"Yeah, but those movies were so far back, it was like the Preakness, those movies were so far back," said Charles Gibson.

(Note: The Preakness is a horse race. In the 2003 Preakness, Funny Cide, a gelding, won the Preakness by nearly ten lengths. I know. I didn't bet on him either.)

"They got my *Matrix* money this weekend, and my popcorn!" chimed in Diane Sawyer. "Yeah. Oh yeah. Absolutely. Couldn't, couldn't wait."

And that was the end of the box office analysis on *Good Morning America*.

The *Los Angeles Times*' 1,131-word article on *Reloaded* included some data analysis that lent perspective to the raw numbers, but the majority of print and broadcast stories that ran in May 2003 just regurgitated those "estimated numbers." And let's not forget, the studios provided the estimates. (It's almost impossible to ascertain "true" box-office figures. Some studio accountants would have you believe that no movie in the history of movies has ever turned a net profit. However, outside sources would later peg the opening weekend for *The Matrix: Reloaded* at about $91.7 million, slightly lower than the studio's figure.) Almost every story printed or broadcast that Monday repeated the "news" that *Reloaded*'s opening weekend was second only to *Spider-Man* and had set a record for an R-rated film, easily besting the $58 million opening weekend of the previous R-rated record-holder, *Hannibal*.

(Less than a year later, in one of the most stunning box office performances in film history, Mel Gibson's *The Passion of the Christ* would soar past *The Matrix: Reloaded* to become the No. 1 R-rated movie of all time on its way to a domestic gross of more than $305 million. Nevertheless, there are no plans for a *Passion* trilogy, even though *The Passion of the Christ: Reloaded* is a promising title.)

Only the trades bothered to point out that *The Matrix: Reloaded* had been crowned with a Neo-like predestiny.

Daily Variety included the all-important information that *Reloaded* had opened in 3,603 venues and that a record 8,517 prints were in circulation, with some multiplexes showing the film on as many as seven screens. (Yet we know there were some moviegoers who walked up to the ticket booths at those multiplexes, right under the marquee saying *The Matrix: Reloaded*, and asked, "Is *Matrix: Reloaded* playing here? How much is it?" It's a wonder these people find their way out of their homes every morning.) An executive with the box-office tracking firm Nielsen EDI told *Variety*, "[*Reloaded*] was running on about one-fourth of all the screens in the country."

In other words, how could it *not* have had a fantastic opening weekend?

Daily Variety and the *Hollywood Reporter* also noted that on one count, *The Matrix: Reloaded* actually bested *Spider-Man*. Its $42.5 million opening-day tally bested *Spidey*'s one-day bow of $39.4 million. Then again, the opening-day figures of *Reloaded* included the late-night Wednesday showings as well as Thursday's numbers, so that's a bit of a cheat too, isn't it? And as we collapse under all these conveniently bent numbers, isn't it becoming apparent that the business of reporting on the business of Hollywood is at best an inexact science?

Average Ticket Prices Over the Last Twenty Years

2003: $6.28
1998: $4.69
1993: $4.19
1988: $4.11
1983: $3.15

Of all the hundreds of stories about the box office for *The Matrix: Reloaded* that ran in the days after the film opened, I couldn't find a single mainstream newspaper or magazine article, and certainly not a TV news transcript, that mentioned such important factors as per-screen average or inflation, aka the stuff that matters. But what good is a second-place all-time finish if it's not a true second-place all-time finish?

When another highly anticipated sci-fi sequel, the *Jurassic Park* follow-up titled *The Lost World*, opened in May 1997, it grossed $72 million in its opening weekend—but that's $91 million in 2003 dollars. *The Lost World* opened on about 325 *fewer* screens than *The Matrix: Reloaded*, meaning its adjusted-for-inflation per-screen average of $27,787 was actually higher than the $25,470 for *Reloaded*.

So on their respective opening weekends, *The Lost World* was a bigger draw than *The Matrix: Reloaded*.

For that matter, the original *Jurassic Park*, released in 1993, has an even higher adjusted per-screen average: $29,230. And while 1989's *Batman* grossed "only" $42.7 million on

2,194 screens, take that same performance, extrapolate it to the year 2003, and give it the platform of the 3,603 screens enjoyed by *Reloaded*, and the Caped Crusader knocks Neo on his ass.

Reporting box-office figures in historical context without taking into account inflation is lazy and stupid. According to conventional wisdom, *Finding Nemo* made more money than *101 Dalmatians*. Yeah, and a 2003 Buick cost more than a 1961 Buick. So what? What matters is if the 2003 Buick is *relatively* more expensive than the 1961 Buick, and if more people have seen *Finding Nemo* in theaters than have seen *101 Dalmatians*. (The answer is no. *Finding Nemo* had a box-office tally of about $340 million, whereas *101 Dalmatians* grossed some $627 million in 2003 dollars. Even though the general population and thus the pool of potential moviegoers has greatly increased in the last thirty-two years, many more people actually bought tickets to see *Dalmatians*.)

Type in the words "Titanic" and "box-office champ" in the Lexis-Nexis database, and nearly 500 stories will pop up. With a domestic gross of $600 million and a worldwide gross of an astonishing $1.8 billion, James Cameron's 1997 film is the undisputed king of the world—the most popular movie ever, by all accounts.

That is, all accounts that don't concern themselves with the actual number of people who have seen a particular film.

When you see a chart of the all-time domestic box-office champions, it goes something like this, give or take a few million:

1. *Titanic* (1997)—$601 million

2. *Star Wars* (1977)—$461 million

3. *Shrek 2* (2004)—$441 million

4. *E.T. The Extra-Terrestrial* (1982)—$435 million

5. *Star Wars Episode 1: The Phantom Menace* (1999)—$431 million

6. *Spider-Man* (2002)—$404 million

7. *The Lord of the Rings: The Return of the King* (2003)—$377 million

8. *Spider-Man 2* (2004)—$374 million

9. *The Passion of the Christ* (2004)—$370 million

10. *Jurassic Park* (1993)—$357 million

The only films on that list released before 1994 are *Star Wars* (1977) and *E.T.* (1982). Gee, maybe that's because as time marches forward, it *costs more to see movies!!!!*

According to Brandon Gray's reliable and invaluable Box Office Mojo web site, these are the all-time domestic box-office champions when the figures are adjusted for inflation:

1. *Gone With the Wind* (1939)—$1.2 billion

2. *Star Wars* (1977)—$1.1 billion

3. *The Sound of Music* (1965)—$874 million

4. *E.T. The Extra-Terrestrial* (1982)—$871 million

5. *The Ten Commandments* (1956)—$804 million

6. *Titanic* (1997)—$788 million

7. *Jaws* (1975)—$786 million

8. *Doctor Zhivago* (1965)—$762 million

9. *The Exorcist* (1973)—$679 million

10. *Snow White and the Seven Dwarfs* (1937)—$669 million

If we're to measure a film's popularity by inflation-adjusted figures, which only makes sense, *The Graduate* was a bigger success than *Forrest Gump*, *The Sting* did a lot more business than *Harry Potter and the Sorcerer's Stone*, and *Sergeant York* outperformed *Top Gun*. Also, *Rear Window* was a bigger hit than *Pretty Woman*, *The Best Years of Our Lives* was a more successful film about World War II than *Saving Private Ryan*, and *The Towering Inferno* generated more business than *The Lord of the Rings: The Two Towers*.

We weren't always obsessed with box-office figures. Twenty years prior to the release of *The Matrix Reloaded*, there was just as much fan anticipation for the *Star Wars* sequel, *Return of the Jedi*, but the media interest (and thus, to a large extent, the public interest) in the film's grosses was much less frantic.

It was a much smaller entertainment-media planet in the early 1980s, before the Internet and such sites as Ain't It Cool News and Box Office Guru; before *Entertainment Tonight* and *Access Hollywood*; before E! and Trio and VH-1; before *Entertainment Weekly* magazine; and before every Sunday night newscast and Monday features section in the country started reporting raw box-office numbers as if they were baseball standings. Twenty years ago, the biggest news organizations were not in the habit of reporting estimated box-office numbers every Monday morning. *Tootsie* was the No. 1 movie in the country for the last three weeks of 1982 and the first six weeks of 1983—a nine-week run that would be virtually impossible to duplicate in today's climate. So it comes as little surprise that between December 1, 1982, and March 1, 1983, the *New York Times* did a number of stories on *Tootsie*, ranging from profiles of its stars to the plausibility of Dustin Hoffman passing as a woman. But there was only one story in the *Times* that focused on the box office: a January 11, 1983, piece about the commercial hits and misses from the recently completed holiday movie season.

Even the record-breaking Memorial Day 1983 performance of *Return of the Jedi* was reported with relaxed restraint. The *New York Times* didn't have a story about the film's huge success until the following Wednesday, June 1. (It ran on Page 20 of Section C.) A check of some 419 transcripts of ABC News programs from May 25, 1983, to June 25, 1983, yielded exactly two mentions of *Jedi*—both coming in stories about a flood in Salt Lake City that caused a 50 percent drop in attendance at a theater showing the movie.

A decade before that, box-office stories were even less frequent, primarily because films were released in a much different manner. Opening weekends have always been a key to a film's success, but there wasn't the make-or-break mentality about the debut weekend that exists today. Films were allowed to grow, to develop, to take on a life of their own through critical acclaim and word of mouth. As recently as the 1980s, even the biggest films would open on several hundred or just over 1,000 theaters, with more screens added as the films built momentum. On various weekends in 1983,

The Big Chill debuted on 722 screens, *Terms of Endearment* on 260 screens and *Flashdance* on 1,140 screens. (*Flashdance* opened at No. 2, but it climbed to No. 1 the following week. Another breakout hit from 1983, *Risky Business*, *never* reached No. 1, but steadily accumulated business over a multi-month run. In today's make-or-break atmosphere, those films probably wouldn't be given the chance to develop a fan base at such a moderate pace. If you don't open with a splash, television advertising and print ads are reduced or eliminated, and the number of screens on which your film is shown will quickly plummet.) In the 2000s, there's so much emphasis placed on the opening weekend numbers that even lesser movies flood theaters when they're released, thus pushing aside smaller and often better films. In 2002, for example, lousy films such as *XXX* (opening on 3,374 screens), *Mr. Deeds* (3,271 screens) and *Scooby-Doo* (3,447 screens) were mortal locks to open at No. 1. Moviegoers hardly had a choice to vote otherwise.

According to a PBS *Frontline* special, "The Monster That Ate Hollywood," until the early 1970s major films would play "for three months or so in only one location before slowly moving into other major cities and then, finally, to second- and third-run theaters in small towns across the country." This policy was first challenged in 1972, when *The Godfather*

opened in 5 theaters on its opening weekend and then expanded to 316 theaters the next week. And then in the summer of 1975, *Jaws* opened in a whopping 465 theaters. The summer blockbuster was born, and as *Jaws* set records left and right, there were stories about the film's financial performance in the mainstream media—just as there would be for the next decade and a half whenever a movie did unusually well. But it wasn't until the late 1980s and early 1990s that estimates of box-office figures were made public on a regular basis. *Daily Variety's* practice of reporting opening weekend estimates began in the summer of 1989, when *Batman* was big news. In the 1990s, as studios started releasing films on 1,500 and then 2,000 and then 3,000 screens, as the Internet took off and publications like *Entertainment Weekly* thrived, the media started running charts based on the figures released by the studios every Sunday.

Studios don't even bother waiting for people to go to the movies on Sunday before they crunch the numbers and hand out their three-day estimates. And with the notable exception of the *Los Angeles Times*, the vast majority of news organizations reports those estimates on Monday and tells us that "final figures" are not yet available—and then never give us those final figures. Why can't the media just wait until Tuesday, when the numbers are at least a bit more accurate? Because we'd rather be first (or at least tied for first) than precise. And in the era of the twenty-four-hour news cycle, by Tuesday the previous weekend's box office numbers are old news.

Not that you have to even wait until Monday to get the weekend box-office estimates. As I write this, it's precisely 2:19 P.M. Central Standard Time on Sunday, March 29, 2004. I'm going to store this document and fiddle around the Internet in search of the latest figures, which I can obtain from Box Office Guru, Box Office Mojo, Yahoo and other sites. Bingo. In the No. 1 slot, God help us all, is *Scooby-Doo 2: Monsters Unleashed*, with $30.7 million, and a per-screen average of $9,282 on 3,212 screens. The next four slots belong to *The Ladykillers*, with $13 million; *The Passion of the Christ*, with $12.4 million; *Dawn of the Dead*, with $10.3 million; and *Jersey Girl*, with $8.3 million. With a tap-tap here and a tap-tap there, I have access to the weekend box-office tallies for four dozen other films, including the percentage change from the previous week, the number of weeks the film has been in theaters and its total gross. This while people are still filing into theaters for the matinee showings of *Scooby-Doo 2* on its third day of release.

Even those Sunday afternoon figures are old news to studio marketing executives, who can usually determine a film's fate by Friday evening or Saturday morning. You can spend a decade developing a script, begging for financial approval, doing the casting, filming, editing and promoting—and it can take less than a day to learn whether you've got a hit or a crushing disappointment on your hands.

A lot of moviegoers are like the movie and TV stars who never go to the Lakers games until the Western Conference Finals: They want to be associated with a winner. When a film opens in first place—even if it's a piece of junk and it almost *had* to open in first place since it's playing on 20 percent of the country's movie screens—the media publish those box-office charts, and the studios take out ads proclaiming, "IT'S THE NUMBER ONE MOVIE IN AMERICA!" Casual movie fans then don their metaphorical "#1" foam fingers and rush out to support the film, because they want to be part of this latest pop-culture phenomenon before it's too late—in other words, before another blockbuster opens in a week or two.

The cycle perpetuates itself. On the weekend of *Scooby Doo 2's* triumph, Michel Gondry's beautifully loopy *Eternal Sunshine of the Spotless Mind*, with an Oscar-worthy performance from Jim Carrey, was the No. 9 film for the weekend with a gross of $5.4 million (and a three-week total of $16.7 million), meaning that it wasn't even on the radar when the newspapers printed the Top Five performers for the weekend. Despite the facts that the *Scooby* sequel's opening take was $24 million less than the debut of the original *Scooby* and that it's appearing on more than twice as many screens as *Eternal Sunshine*, the media hailed *Scooby* as the weekend's big winner—and hardly anybody even mentioned *Eternal Sunshine*.

The hits get bigger and the underdogs get buried—and quality loses out.

Some excellent and overlooked films from the last five years, and their disappointing theatrical box-office tallies (all figures from Box Office Mojo web site):

2 0 0 4

Spartan (written and directed by David Mamet, starring Val Kilmer): $4.4 million

The Dreamers (directed by Bernardo Bertolucci): $2.5 million

Silver City (directed by John Sayles): $1.1 million

Young Adam (starring Ewan McGregor): $770,000

2 0 0 3

Elephant (directed by Gus Van Sant): $1.26 million

The Shape of Things (directed by Neil Labute, starring Paul Rudd and Rachel Weisz): $736,000

Assassination Tango (directed by and starring Robert Duvall): $1.03 million

The Dancer Upstairs (directed by John Malkovich, starring Javier Bardem): $2.4 million

Owning Mahowny (starring Philip Seymour Hoffman and Minnie Driver): $1 million

City of Ghosts (directed by and starring Matt Dillon): $357,000

2 0 0 2

Lantana (starring Anthony LaPaglia): $4.6 million

The Grey Zone (directed by Tim Blake Nelson, starring Mira Sorvino, David Arquette and Steve Buscemi): $537,000

2 0 0 1

Mulholland Dr. (directed by David Lynch, starring Naomi Watts and Laura Elena Harring): $7.2 million

Dinner Rush (starring Danny Aiello, John Corbett and Sandra Bernhard): $638,000

Diamond Men (starring Robert Forster, Donnie Wahlberg and Jasmine Guy): $191,000

2 0 0 0

State and Main (directed by David Mamet, starring William H. Macy, Alec Baldwin and Sarah Jessica Parker): $6.9 million

Requiem for a Dream (directed by Darren Aronofsky, starring Jared Leto and Jennifer Connelly): $3.6 million

Cradle Will Rock (directed by Tim Robbins, starring John Cusack, Susan Sarandon, Vanessa Redgrave): $2.9 million

1 9 9 9

Ride with the Devil (directed by Ang Lee, starring Tobey Maguire, Skeet Ulrich and Jewel): $635,000

Sunshine (starring Ralph Fiennes and Rachel Weisz): $5 million

Another Day in Paradise (starring James Woods and Melanie Griffith): $1 million

Confessions of a Dangerous Mind is a rare example of a theatrical misfire that was given a re-release by the studio. Recognizing that the quirky comedy/thriller was buried in the avalanche of 2002 holiday releases, Miramax put the film back in theaters in late summer 2003. Unfortunately, it grossed less than $100,000 before disappearing, again.

The Envelope. Please.

When people ask me if I get to attend the Academy Awards every year, my answer is yes.

And no.

Yes, I'm on the site at Hollywood and Highland for the event—and like almost every other journalist from around the world who covers the Oscars, I'm clad in formal wear, which is more than a little stupid when you think about it. I didn't have to don a Bulls uniform when I covered dozens of games during Michael Jordan's championship runs in the 1990s, and I didn't have to wear a navy-blue politicians' suit when I reported on the Democratic convention in Chicago in 1996 or the Clinton impeachment hearings in Washington in 1998, and I sure as hell didn't have to mirror the attire of firefighters and cops in my days as a city reporter for the *Chicago Sun-Times*—so why am I required to dress up like a fifth-rate George Clooney wannabe for the Oscars? It's one thing for Maria Menounos to hit the red carpet in a shimmering gown and a $400 hairstyle. But what's the point in me, or a features reporter from the *Orange County Register*, or for that matter some manner-challenged and amazingly sweaty guy from a European-based fanzine who's a member of the Hollywood Foreign Press, schlepping around in a tuxedo on the fringes of the event for eight hours?

Which brings me to the "no" part of that Oscars reply. Sure, the fine folks at the Academy of Motion Pictures Arts and Sciences give me an all-access pass and a Mac-daddy front row seat in the metal bleachers for the wonderfully garish red-carpet parade. (With the exception of the 2003 awards, of course, when the red carpet proceedings were eliminated as a gesture of support for the American troops in Iraq, who almost certainly didn't give a shit whether Nicole Kidman stood on a carpet on Hollywood Boulevard, preened for the cameras and deflected idiotic questions from an increasingly addled Joan Rivers.) But there's no room for the media at the Oscars themselves. The Kodak Theatre has a capacity of 3,500, and there are some 5,700 members of the Academy—so every year more than 2,000 bona-fide voters can't get tickets. Even some past winners and nominees probably couldn't get into the building: At this point, does an F. Murray Abraham or a Mira Sorvino rate two ducats on the main floor? Probably not.

So once the red carpet proceedings draw to a close and the last star has been seated and the ceremony itself is about to begin, all the credentialed journalists are herded out of sight and backstage. Well, beyond backstage. We're actually in a series of banquet rooms at the Renaissance Hollywood Hotel, adjacent to the Kodak Theatre. Print and radio reporters in one room, TV correspondents in another, photographers in yet another. There's a big-ass buffet set up in the hallway just past the security X-ray machines. Every time you go to the bathroom, you have to pass through the security checkpoint in order to reenter the press area, lest some reporter try to pull a Michael Corleone and hide a weapon in the men's room. (At the 2004 Oscars, a red-faced Joel Siegel threw a major tantrum at the security checkpoint, even invoking the f-bomb as he berated a public relations woman. Maybe he was upset over some soggy shrimp cocktail.)

I'm usually in the oversized pen reserved for print and radio media, where there are several rows of long tables arranged *Harry Potter* banquet hall–style. The tables are equipped with telephones and jacks and outlets for computers, and the uncomfortable folding chairs are spaced about two inches apart. At the front of the room is a makeshift stage for the winners—a simple but sturdy platform with a temporary curtain festooned with the Oscar logo, the backdrop you see in all those newspaper photos of the winners holding their trophies. (In papers like *USA Today*, the Supporting Actor and Supporting Actress winners usually get the front-page treatment, because the deadlines come before the big winners are announced.)

Watching the Oscars backstage is an exercise in controlled chaos. The feed of the ABC-TV broadcast can be viewed on several monitors spaced throughout the room, but as the winners are funneled in from the Kodak Theatre to talk to the press, the sound from the broadcast is muted so we can ask the freshly minted winner such probing questions as "How do you feel!" and "Congratulations, how do you feel!" In order to keep up with the audio of the live telecast, journalists are given wireless headsets (they work pretty well if you don't move your head around too much), giving the room a kind of United Nations–knockoff feel. Sometimes a star will be in the middle of answering a question when the next award is announced and applause will erupt in the press box. Or a winner answering questions will catch a glimpse of the telecast-in-progress on a monitor and interrupt herself to say, "Hold on, I want to see who wins here!" Adding to the general headache-inducing cacophony of the experience are the scattered loudmouth radio reporters who periodically feed updates to their audiences with all the subtlety and nuance of a boom box on a cigarette boat in Miami Beach.

So you've got the winners talking onstage, the audio of the live broadcast pumping through the headset, and the radio reporters providing updates in English, Spanish, Italian, French, Japanese, etc. The net effect is like listening to four radio stations and watching TV at the same time for nearly four hours. Advil anyone?

At the 2003 Academy Awards, the announcement of *Bowling for Columbine* as the winner of Best Documentary was met with great cheers in the pressroom. (If you're a reporter and you cheer in the press box at a sporting event, you'll be mocked for life. Cheer in the gallery at a Chicago city council meeting and you'll be roughed up in an alley. But at the Academy Awards, the announcement of each winner is met with applause, shouts of glee and the occasional wail of disappointment. The winners receive hearty ovations when they come backstage to meet the press with their gleaming golden trophy-boys in hand. I've even seen one old gossip hen leap from her seat to embrace an Oscar winner like a long-lost child.) The room went quiet as Michael Moore took the stage, accompanied by the other nominees, and he launched into an almost verbatim version of the speech he had given the day before at the Independent Spirit Awards in Santa Monica. As the cheers in the Kodak Theatre gave way to a strong wave of boos, most of us in the pressroom were rubbing our hands together in glee. It was that rare and spicy thing known as a controversial Academy Awards moment! This was Sacheen Littlefeather accepting on behalf of Marlon Brando, this was Vanessa Redgrave talking about "Zionist hoodlums," this was a streaker interrupting David Niven, this was Sally Field working out her self-esteem issues in public, this was Oscar history!

I have a theory that a lot of movie critics and reporters have a particular affection for Michael Moore because a lot of them look like Michael Moore. Plus they share his liberal viewpoint. They're under the illusion that he's one of them, even though he's really a wealthy, famous and egocentric star. Imagine how disappointing it was for the movie media when Moore came backstage after one of the most divisive acceptance speeches in Oscar history and tried to bully them into accepting his instant revisionist history. According to Moore, only "five people" had booed him, and it would be irresponsible for us to claim otherwise.

"Do your jobs!" he commanded us.

Will do, Mr. Free Speech. Let's start with this fact: A lot more than five people booed you. A lot more.

into accepting his instant revisionist history. According to Moore, only "five people" had booed him, and it would be irresponsible for us to claim otherwise.

As much as I admire Moore for facing the world in his most glorious moment and speaking his mind, knowing full well that he'd be alienating and offending millions, the actual speech he delivered was an uneasy mix of Craig Kilborn–level stand-up jokes and grammatically wretched hyperbole—not to mention inappropriate timing that probably did more harm than good to his cause.

Moore invited the other nominees in the documentary category onstage with him, and then pointed out that he and the other filmmakers appreciate nonfiction despite living "in fictitious times . . . where we have fictitious election results . . . and a fictitious president." He continued his speech with a rant against the war in Iraq, bizarrely citing the fiction of duct tape and orange alerts and concluding, "Shame on you, Mr. Bush, shame on you. And any time you got the Pope and the Dixie Chicks against you, your time is up. Thank you very much!"

Well now. Those are some pretty specious and fictitious arguments. Of course Bush did declare war for "fictitious" reasons, but it had little to do with orange alerts and duct tape, and everything to do with connecting Saddam Hussein to 9/11 and making claims about weapons of mass destruction. Beyond that, you'd think the left-wing Moore would say that any time you've got the Pope and the Dixie Chicks against you, you're doing something *right*. The joke doesn't really work. And when Moore said, "We are against this war," who was he talking about? Was he referring to his fellow documentary makers, whom he had invited onstage? Was he presuming to speak for the nation?

There was a lot of emotion behind Moore's speech, and he did a credible job of acting as if it had all come to him in that moment, even though he'd given the same speech at an awards ceremony in Santa Monica just twenty-four hours earlier—but under the cold light of history, the speech teeters badly.

Moore's talents as documentarian are undeniable, but those skills pale in comparison to his ability to generate publicity. In May 2004, he scored a Page One story in the *New York Times* and tons of international attention with his claim that Disney was "censoring" his anti-Bush documentary, *Fahrenheit 9/11*. Of course, it's only censorship when a government body suppresses free speech—not when a corporation makes a business decision. In the weeks leading up to the June 25 theatrical release of *Fahrenheit 9/11*, Moore was in the news nearly every day, whether he was claiming that he had knowledge of the Iraqi prisoner torture scandal months before most of the country heard about it, showcasing the film for high-profile audiences, or lamenting the fact that the movie was given an "R" rating. Not that there's anything wrong with this. Moore is a master showman, but he's also a great patriot and one of the most important filmmakers of his generation. *Fahrenheit 9/11* is a film that every American should have seen.

The same could be said of Halle Berry's highly emotional speech at the 2002 Academy Awards. Her intent was pure and sincere, but her actual words were kind of wacky.

"Oh my God," said Berry. "I'm sorry. This moment is so much bigger than me. This moment is for Dorothy Dandridge, Lena Horne, Diahann Carroll. It's for the women that stand beside me—Jada Pinkett, Angela Bassett, and it's for every nameless, faceless woman of color that now has a chance because this door tonight has been opened. Thank you. I'm so honored and thank the Academy for choosing me to be the vessel from which this blessing might flow."

That's what happens when you wear such a revealing dress. Blessings flow from your vessel.

After thanking her manager, her mother, her husband and her stepdaughter, in that order, Berry thanked Lion's Gate Films and assorted people associated with the film. By that time, she was struggling not to hyperventilate.

"I—who else—I have so many people that I know I need to thank, um, my lawyer, Neil Meyer. Thank you, okay wait a minute, I gotta take this, seventy-four years here! Okay, I've gotta take this time. I gotta thank my lawyer Neil Meyer for making this deal."

Halle! You remind us that seventy-four years passed before an African-American woman won a Best Actress award—and then you thank your *lawyer for making the deal*? We shall overcome—at a billable rate of $300 an hour.

Berry went on to thank Spike Lee, Oprah Winfrey and Warren Beatty before she finished with a chorus of "Thank you, thank you, thank you!" Not since Gwyneth "*Shakespeare in Love*" Paltrow sobbed like a beauty pageant winner had there been such a disproportionate amount of tears and emotion. If you expend that much emotion on winning an award for acting, what do you do on your wedding day or when your first child is born? Fly?

Or maybe you just name the kid Apple.

Not that Halle and Gwyneth have the market cornered on Oscar acceptance speeches that sound lovely and touch our hearts but amount to nothing more than pretty gobbledygook. When the great Tom Hanks won Best Actor for his portrayal of a lawyer with AIDS in *Philadelphia* (a fine performance, but the Oscar really should have gone to Denzel Washington, who had the more challenging, juicier and complex role as the homophobic ambulance-chaser who represents the AIDS patient), he moved a worldwide audience to tears with a speech that started out cryptic and got weirder. Hanks began by referencing "Streets of Philadelphia," the Bruce Springsteen song that had been performed by Neil Young. Then he mentioned Rita Wilson, his spouse.

"I could not be standing here without the undying love that was just in the ballad, not by Bruce, but by Neil Young, and I have that in a lover that is so close to find we should all be able to experience such heaven right here on Earth."

Hanks went on to thank the actor who played his lover in the film: "And a cast that includes Antonio Banderas, who, second to my lover, is the only person I would trade for."

So I guess Hanks was saying he wouldn't trade anyone for Rita Wilson, but Antonio was a close second.

Next on Hanks' laundry list of thanks were his high school drama teacher and a former classmate—both gay. (This part of the speech was the inspiration for *In & Out*, starring Matt Dillon as an award-winning actor who "outs" his gay teacher, played by Kevin Kline.) After naming the former teacher and the former classmate, Hanks then delivered one of the most memorable monologues in Oscar's long history:

> And there lies my dilemma here tonight. I know that my work in this case is magnified by the fact that the streets of heaven are too crowded with angels. We know their names. They number a thousand for each of the red ribbons we wear tonight. They finally rest in the warm embrace of the Creator of us all, a healing embrace that cools their fevers, clears their skin, and allows their eyes to see the simple self-evident common-sense truth that is made manifest by the benevolent Creator of

us all, and was written down on paper by wise men, tolerant men, in the city of Philadelphia two hundred years ago. God bless you all, God have mercy on us all, and God bless America.

How many among us were moved to tears by Hanks' pure and true words? Would it be an exaggeration to say that millions of people all over the world cried at once? I don't think so, and you can count me among their ranks. But as I look at that passage now, and as I urge you to reread it, I can only wonder: What the hell was Hanks saying? I mean, I know he's paying tribute to those who had died of AIDS, and he was offering a hope and a prayer that somewhere in the skies, a higher power had accepted those victims into his eternal embrace and had eliminated their suffering—but this speech has major problems. First, what dilemma? He just won the Academy Award, he didn't have no stinkin' dilemma! Then there was Hanks' heartfelt and moving but uninformed reference to AIDS victims as "angels." According to conventional religious doctrine, angels are not the spirits of deceased human beings, they're celestial creatures that never walked the Earth, ranked according to a specific hierarchy of powers. As for "the simple self-evident truth that is made manifest by the benevolent Creator of us all," that means, well, nothing, though it seems to be an attempt to meld the Declaration of Independence and the Bible. And though Hanks should be commended for trying to connect the title of his film with the founding fathers of this country, I'm not so sure those wise and tolerant men would be all that understanding about a gay lawyer who picked up AIDS from a one-night stand, given that they couldn't find room for blacks or women when they were writing things down in Philadelphia some 200 years ago.

But hey. Hanks' speech was emotionally effective, and the sentiments he tried to convey were undoubtedly genuine. This is probably the foremost example of an Oscar acceptance speech that resonates with millions—even though not a one of us could actually recite the lines verbatim, or explain exactly what Hanks was talking about.

12 Things That Can Be Done to Improve the Academy Awards

1. Ease pedestrian traffic on the red carpet. There has to be a better way to herd the nominees and presenters into the Kodak Theatre without creating a celebrity traffic jam every year.

2. Ban inappropriate choreography. Can we ever forget the horror that was the *Saving Private Ryan* dance number? Can we enact legislation to make sure it'll never happen again?

3. Fix the medley of dead people. Every year they show a montage of actors and behind-the-scenes artists

who have left this mortal coil since the last Academy Awards—and every year it turns into a macabre popularity contest, with the audience cheering enthusiastically for popular favorites, and murmuring, "Who's that?" when lesser known figures are shown: "I never heard of that old dude, was he in Westerns or something? . . . oh there's Gregory Peck, I loved him!"

They don't have to drop the dead-people medley— just mute the audio in the theater, so we don't have to bear those awkward moments when hardly anyone applauds for some wonderful and talented but long-forgotten costume designer who died at ninety-four.

4. In "lesser" categories such as Documentary Short and Animated Short, read the nominees and announce the winners—but instead of inviting the winners onstage, have them stand up and take a bow, and then escort them backstage where they can pick up their Oscars. All due respect to these people, but nobody knows who you are and nobody has seen your work and nobody knows anyone you're thanking.

5. Memo to all nominees: Prepare a friggin' speech! Don't get up there and fumble around while you rummage through your pockets for the notes you scribbled on a napkin five minutes ago. If you can't write something yourself, have a scriptwriter friend help you out, because if you go up there unprepared and you rely on the emotion of the moment, you are going to greatly increase your chances of profound, worldwide embarrassment. For every Adrien Brody who makes out with Halle Berry on the spur of the moment, there's an Al Pacino who hems and haws and sputters, reminding us that all actors, even the best ones, are at the mercy of the words they speak.

6. As was the case in 2004, continue to give the major-category winners more time to speak. There's no reason why the winner for Best Editing and the winner for Best Actor should be given the same time limit.

7. Whenever possible, hire Steve Martin to host.

8. If Billy Crystal returns as host, require him to come up with some new bits. The footage of Crystal "appearing" in the nominated films is technically impressive, but the joke is wearing thin. As for the musical medley that follows, again, it used to be funny, but it's become awfully predictable. Shouldn't the humor go beyond the limits of a Weird Al Yankovich routine?

9. When the show is over, instead of a quick good-bye, keep the cameras running like they do on C-SPAN so we can see the winners basking in the glow of victory, the losers smiling painfully and everyone else making a beeline for the Governors' Ball or the restrooms.

10. If you're going to ask any legend past the age of seventy-five to present or receive an award, spend a little time with the legend beforehand to make sure he or she is up to the task and won't be embarrassed on live television.

11. Replace that boring-ass orchestra with a hip, fun all-star rock/pop band led by Paul Shaffer.

12. Hold a worldwide lottery and select ten lucky winners who will be allowed to attend the red carpet festivities, the awards and the Governors Ball. On the most important night of the year for the people who make movies, there should be room to acknowledge and thank the people who *go* to movies.

Every once in awhile you'll hear about someone attempting to sell an Academy Award statuette on eBay or through an auction house such as Sotheby's or Christie's—but only the trophies awarded up to 1949 can be sold for profit. Since 1950, every winner has had to sign an agreement stating that before placing an Oscar on the auction block, the winner (or the person who has inherited the statue) must give the Academy the right to purchase the statue back for $1.

From the official Academy Awards rulebook, here's the text of the agreement that has been signed by everyone from Frank Sinatra to Halle Berry.

Gentlemen:

I hereby acknowledge receipt from you of a replica of your copyrighted statuette, commonly known as the "Oscar," as an award for achievement in motion picture arts and sciences. I acknowledge that my receipt of said replica does not entitle me to any right whatever in your copyright, trademark and service mark of said statuette and that only the physical replica itself shall belong to me. In consideration of delivering said replica to me, I agree to comply with your rules and regulations respecting its use and not to sell or otherwise dispose of it, nor permit it to be sold or disposed of by operation of law, without first offering to sell it for the sum of $1. You shall have thirty days after any such offer is made to you within which to accept it. . . .

MOST DISAPPOINTING CAREERS AFTER WINNING THE ACADEMY AWARD

F. Murray Abraham,
BEST ACTOR FOR *AMADEUS*, 1984

Subsequent duds: *The Bonfire of the Vanities, By the Sword, National Lampoon's Loaded Weapon 1, Last Action Hero, Muppets From Space, Mimic, 13 Ghosts*

Roberto Benigni,
BEST ACTOR FOR *LIFE IS BEAUTIFUL*, 1998

Subsequent dud of epic proportions: *Pinocchio*

Louise Fletcher,
BEST ACTRESS FOR *ONE FLEW OVER THE CUCKOO'S NEST*, 1975

Subsequent duds: *The Lady in Red, Mamma Dracula, Two-Moon Junction, Return to Two Moon Junction, High School High*

Cher,
BEST ACTRESS FOR *MOONSTRUCK*, 1987

Subsequent duds: *Faithful, Tea with Mussolini*

George Chakiris,
BEST SUPPORTING ACTOR FOR *WEST SIDE STORY*,
1961

Subsequent duds: *Two and Two Make Six* (aka *The Girl Swappers*), *Why Not Stay for Breakfast?*

Cuba Gooding Jr.,
BEST SUPPORTING ACTOR FOR *JERRY MAGUIRE*,
1996

Subsequent duds: *What Dreams May Come, Pearl Harbor, Rat Race, Snow Dogs, Boat Trip, The Fighting Temptations, Radio*

Whoopi Goldberg,
BEST SUPPORTING ACTRESS FOR *GHOST*, 1990

Subsequent duds: *Boys on the Side, Eddie, MonkeyBone*

Mira Sorvino,
BEST SUPPORTING ACTRESS FOR *MIGHTY APHRODITE*, 1995

Subsequent duds: *Tales of Erotica, Mimic, Wisegirls, Gods and Generals*

Once upon a time, nominees, presenters and performers at awards shows were given relatively inexpensive tokens like embroidered jackets, T-shirts, gift certificates and maybe a scented candle or a box of chocolates. But in recent years, the so-called goodie basket has become more of a goodie sleigh, brimming with obscenely priced luxury items. In the days leading up to the 2003 Academy Awards, a lot of stars talked about how inappropriate it would be to parade up and down the red carpet or party into the night, what with that bothersome war in Iraq and everything—but apparently that collective crisis of conscience didn't extend to the least bit of angst over accepting perhaps the gaudiest goodie basket in award-show history. (Until the 2004 Oscars, that is.) It would have been a great PR move if one of the recipients had declined the booty or had sent $30,000 worth of useful items in a big-ass goodie basket to the men and women overseas. Didn't happen.

A partial listing of the contents of the 2003 Academy Awards goodie basket, with estimated retail value:

Gift certificate from Morton's Steakhouse: $1,500

Nicole Miller cashmere halter top: $350

Oliveri Fashion shirt: $300

Omas 360 rolling ball blue resin pen: $250

Bloomsbury crystal compact: $275

Valerie Beverly Hills silver vanity makeup kit: $3,000

> Revlon "Red Carpet Bag" filled with cosmetics: $1,000
> Fendi stainless steel wristwatch: $1,000
> Stuart Weitzman shoes: $500
> Sports Club bicoastal membership: $4,000
> Gaiam sheets: $475
> Timmy Woods of Beverly Hills evening bag: $500
> Estée Lauder Oscar Spa package, including Manolo Blahnik sandals, Hermès beach towel, Estée Lauder cosmetics, Veuve Clicquot champagne, etc.: $15,000
> Rosewood's Badrutt's Palace Hotel gift certificate: $1,500

In 2004, the total value of the items in Academy Awards goodie baskets soared to $110,000, with such high-end "trinkets" as a $6,000 wide-screen TV; a $10,000 stay at Caesars Palace in Las Vegas that included gambling chips and tickets to see Celine Dion; two business-class tickets from Los Angeles to Auckland, New Zealand; a $500 espresso machine; and a seven-day cruise in the Mediterranean or Caribbean.

HANDICAPPING THE OSCARS

Oscar has always had a soft spot for characters who are physically disabled, deeply troubled, or both—and it doesn't hurt your chances if you play a guy who winds up dead or causing someone's death. Over the last decade and a half, the Best Actor category has been dominated by portrayals that fit one or more of the above categories.

The actors, their movies and their problems:

1988: Dustin Hoffman, *Rain Man*, autistic.

1989: Daniel Day-Lewis, *My Left Foot*, cerebral palsy.

1990: Jeremy Irons, *Reversal of Fortune*, slimy accused murderer.

1991: Anthony Hopkins, *The Silence of the Lambs*, murderous cannibal.

1992: Al Pacino, *Scent of a Woman*, blind, alcoholic and suicidal.

1993: Tom Hanks, *Philadelphia*, dies of AIDS.

1994: Tom Hanks, *Forrest Gump*, mentally challenged.

1995: Nicolas Cage, *Leaving Las Vegas*, alcoholic who deliberately drinks himself to death.

1996: Geoffrey Rush, *Shine*, mental illness.

1997: Jack Nicholson, *As Good As It Gets*, obsessive-compulsive.

1998: Roberto Benigni, *Life is Beautiful*, killed in concentration camp.

1999: Kevin Spacey, *American Beauty*, murdered by neighbor.

2000: Russell Crowe, *Gladiator*, killed in battle arena.

2001: Denzel Washington, *Training Day*, hard-drinking, drug-taking, law-breaking cop, shot and killed.

2002: Adrien Brody, *The Pianist*. For the first time
since Michael Douglas in *Wall Street* (1987),
the Oscar goes to an actor playing someone
who doesn't have a severe emotional or
physical affliction, or a date with mortality.
(Of course, Douglas' character does wind up
in jail, and Brody's character narrowly
survives the Holocaust.)

2003: Sean Penn, *Mystic River*, ex-con, daughter is
murdered, exacts violent revenge on alleged
killer of his daughter.

THE GOLDEN GLOBES

For all the perennial and legitimate complaints about the
Academy Awards ceremony—too long, too structured, too
stodgy, too self-important, too many commercials, too many
reaction shots of Jack Nicholson grinning from behind his
sunglasses—the Oscar itself is unquestionably the most prestigious honor in the movie world, and for that matter in the
entirety of this business we call show. (And there are a lot of
awards shows these days. According to *Daily Variety*, we now
have more awards programs than there are days in the year.)

So what's the second biggest film awards program? What
honor is considered so important that studios will take out
ads to trumpet its winners? If an actor or filmmaker could
win anything *other* than an Academy Award, what would
most of them opt for?

The answer to all of the above is: the Golden Globes.

In January 2004, the NBC telecast of the Golden Globes

drew 26.7 million viewers. That's about 17 million less than the Nielsen ratings for the 2003 Academy Awards (held in February 2004), but it's 9 million more viewers than the broadcast of the 2003 Emmys. In fact the Globes regularly outdraw the Emmys and the Tonys *combined.*

The celebrity attendance rate at the Globes is equal to that of the Oscars, with the major nominees shined and buffed and ready to leap onstage and say, "Wow! This is *such* a surprise!" In fact the celeb ratio may be even greater at the Globes than the Oscars, as the Globes has separate categories for Drama and Musical/Comedy, meaning there are more nominees—not to mention the TV-world candidates, some of whom are paired up with big-time movie stars, e.g., Jennifer Aniston and Brad Pitt.

When the winners' names are called, they're absolutely thrilled, and they're often shaking and weeping as they thank God, the Hollywood Foreign Press Association, their spouses and their agents, not necessarily in that order. It's a major, major moment.

Everyone in the media from *Access Hollywood* to the *New York Times* makes a big deal out of the Globes, which are routinely credited with having a major influence on the Academy Award nominations. (In 2004, the Oscars were moved from late March to late February, in part because the Academy was tired of the Globes stealing its thunder. Now the Globes are given out after the Oscar nominations have been closed—but voting for the Oscar winner remains open. So that means that if a Golden Globe winner happens to be an Academy Award nominee, he or she is immediately touted as the "favorite" for the Oscar.) The show itself is a hit with TV critics and fans because it's more relaxed and spontaneous than the Academy Awards. No one ever has to come running from the bathroom to accept an Oscar, à la Christine Lahti at the Golden Globes in 1998.

The Hollywood Foreign Press Association does know how to throw a party, and it's always fun to watch famous people pining for awards as they sit at tables crowded with picked-over salmon filets and half-empty champagne bottles. It's like a grown-up version of the prom—except *everybody* looks like the king and queen. The chances of seeing a tipsy star doing something truly goofy are much greater than at the Oscars. That said, let us not forget one important thing about the Golden Globes:

They're a farce.

The Golden Globes aren't quite the joke they used to be—but that's like saying Lake Erie isn't as polluted as it used to be. (And as goofy as they are, the Globes aren't quite as silly as the People's Choice Awards. In 2004, the People's Choice nominees for Favorite Motion Picture Actor were Johnny Depp, Denzel Washington and Mel Gibson. The winner was Gibson, who hadn't appeared in a single film in 2003. And in 1999, *Seinfeld* was honored as the People's Choice Award winner for favorite TV comedy series—a year after it had gone off the air.

"We're not making any more shows!" Jerry Seinfeld pointed out in a taped acceptance speech.) The Globes were founded in 1944 by a small band of foreign journalists who declared *The Song of Bernadette* the Best Picture of the Year at a luncheon held in the commissary of 20th Century–Fox Studios. The Golden Globes (as they were officially titled a year later) always had a reputation as a fun evening where the stars could relax and hang loose, but the general public barely noticed the ceremony until the late 1950s and early 1960s, when it first started appearing on television. The Globes made their TV debut on Los Angeles station KTTV, with the always-dynamic Andy Williams hosting, and in the 1960s went national as part of Williams' show on NBC. In 1966, NBC signed a five-year deal with the Hollywood Foreign Press Association to broadcast the Globes as a ninety-minute special.

One of the more interesting moments in Globe history occurred in 1967, when Sally *"The Flying Nun"* Field was suspended on wires and flew across the audience. Upon her exit, she reportedly ran into some technical difficulties. "Field . . . dangled near the ceiling for the better part of the evening," reported *Newsday*.

By that time, questions were being raised about the integrity of the Globes. One persistent rumor said winners were tipped off in advance so they'd be more likely to show up at the ceremony. News reports from the time said that *Bonnie and Clyde* was snubbed by the Hollywood Foreign Press Association because of concerns about its violent content. And, according to *Newsday*, when Frank Sinatra said he couldn't be bothered to show up to receive something called the World Favorite Film Award in 1967, the HFPA did a recount and discovered that the "real" winner was Paul Newman, who coincidentally *had* agreed to show up and pick up his trophy. (Given that the HFPA has never had as many as 100 members, one might legitimately wonder how the tally could have been screwed up in the first place.)

In 1968, after the Federal Communications Commission questioned the voting procedures, NBC dropped the Golden Globes. Four years later, KTTV again gave the Globes a TV home and syndicated the broadcast to about two dozen markets. Through much of the 1970s, the Globes were shown via syndication, with some markets going live and others showing it on a one-day taped delay. The ceremony returned to NBC in 1977 as a taped, two-hour special. But a year later the show was "dark" again, this time due to insufficient sponsorship. No one, it seemed, took the Globes seriously.

By the early 1980s, the Globes had moved to CBS—and the HFPA was still under fire. The credentials of its approximately eighty members were routinely called into question. The Globes reached their nadir in 1981 with the infamous Pia Zadora affair, when most of the membership was flown to Las Vegas as guests of Zadora's wealthy and older husband, Meshulam Riklis. A few short weeks later, the HFPA shamelessly crowned Zadora as "New Star of the Year in a Motion Picture" for her work in the unwatchable flop *Butterfly*, thus claiming they believed she showed more promise than the losing nominees: Kathleen Turner in *Body Heat*, Craig Wasson in *Four Friends*, Rachel Ward for *Sharky's Machine* and Howard E. Rollins Jr. and Elizabeth McGovern in *Ragtime*. (In 1982, the New Star award was split by gender. Ben Kingsley won for *Gandhi*, and Sandahl Bergman won for *Conan the Barbarian*. The following year, the category was dropped.) For a modern-day equivalent, this would be like Ashton Kutcher beating out Scarlett Johansson, Orlando Bloom, Keira Knightley, the Gyllenhaal siblings and the kids from *Whale Rider* and *In America* as Best New Talent.

Shortly after the Zadora debacle, CBS dropped the Golden Globes, and it was back to the world of syndication and taped-delay broadcasts. Cable station TBS picked up the show in the late 1980s, and it returned to NBC in 1995—but the criticism never really abated. In 1993, director Rob Reiner complained to the *New York Times* about HFPA "press conferences" that were nothing more than glorified photo-ops for its members. In 1996 the *Washington Post* published a devastating exposé that noted, "[M]ost of [the HFPA's] 88 active members are not full-time journalists, but part-time freelancers for small publications in places like Lithuania and Bangladesh, and include a college professor, a retired engineer, a man who runs an 'auto referral service,' and another who until recently sold appliances in Burbank." The article quoted a former president of the HFPA who said the organization had "about 25 very good, important journalists," with the rest being part-timers writing "four or . . . five articles" a year for relatively obscure publications. But, said the *Post*, some HFPA members couldn't even produce an article every couple of months.

Among those temporarily dropped from the ranks for lack of journalistic production was one Dagmar Dunlevy—but Dunlevy was reinstated to the HFPA in 1997 and was eventually named president of the organization, gaining a kind of minor celebritydom as an oft-quoted and photographed spokesperson for the Globes. (Dunlevy is now the chairman of the board of directors.) Dunlevy regularly writes for *Flare*, the Canadian monthly, and her articles often include a shot of her smiling in a candid snapshot with the subject of her profiles. In a November 2001 Q-and-A interview with Johnny Depp, Dunlevy's probing interview included the following questions and statements:

"You're a devoted father. What did you learn from your parents?"

"You're often featured in magazines' most beautiful people issues. What's your definition of beauty?"

"[Javier Bardem] said you have a great ass."

"But back to beautiful you."

"How's your French coming along?"

"Has a movie ever made you cry?"

And we wonder why Johnny Depp chooses to hide in France and keep his hair in front of his face most of the time rather than schmoozing with junketeer journalists.

In another *Flare* magazine profile, Dunlevy chatted up

Golden Globe winner Madonna and said, "You are so many things: singer, songwriter, mother, lover, actor, icon, role model. What does it take to get there?"

One would have excused Madonna for getting up and saying, "Who cares what it took to get there, the important thing is that I *am* there, which means I don't have to endure nonsense like this." Or she could have said, "You know, I'm not *the* Madonna, so can we ease up a bit with the icon/role model stuff?" But for the record, Ms. Ciccone's actual response was, "It requires a lot of energy, a lot of focus, a lot of discipline. The ability to multi-task. Curiosity. I'm curious about a lot of things."

I'm curious about a lot of things too. Like why the Golden Globes are taken so seriously when the voting is done by approximately ninety cliquish, junketeering entertainment reporters who have to produce only a handful of articles per year in order to remain in good standing with the HFPA.

The answer, of course, is television. When NBC reacquired the Golden Globes and turned the ceremony into a live, three-hour, prime-time special, it was like giving the thing an extreme makeover. Tens of millions of viewers tuned in to see their favorite stars in sparkling gowns and crisp tuxedos (or in some cases, sparkling tuxedos and crisp gowns), and they couldn't be blamed for thinking the Globes were legitimate. Why else would Jack and Gwyneth and Denzel and Tom and Julia show up? And with the entertainment press constantly telling us that the Globes are like the primaries to the Oscars' general election, the Globes' stock just keeps on rising. At this point the Golden Globes are firmly ensconced in the national consciousness as the most important and prestigious award this side of Oscar. But you can't take a delete key to history, and there are those who will never forget Pia Zadora.

Although the Golden Globes are often credited with being the most accurate barometer of the Academy Awards, the eclectic HFPA has often nominated some curious films and performers. Granted, the Globes have separate categories for Drama and Musical/Comedy, but still, some of these Globe nominees are pretty goofy.

Best Picture Nominees

Men in Black, 1997

Legally Blonde, 2001

Analyze This, 1999

The Horse Whisperer, 1998

Patch Adams, Still Crazy and *There's Something About Mary*, 1998

Sabrina, 1995

Nell, 1994

City Slickers, 1991

Some of the more surprising acting nominees in recent years include Billy Crystal for *Mr. Saturday Night*, Arnold Schwarzenegger for *Junior*, Marion Ross for *The Evening Star* and Sandra Bullock for *Miss Congeniality*.

Each year the HFPA selects a "Miss Golden Globe" to act as a kind of Vanna White for the awards. And sometimes they have a "Mister Golden Globe" too. The very first Miss Golden Globe, in 1973, was Kelly Miles, daughter of Vera Miles, and in most years the title has gone to a showbiz kid. Some of the Miss Golden Globes—and a certain Mr. Golden Globe of 1996—have gone on to have film careers of their own.

1975: Melanie Griffith (Tippi Hedren)

1978: Elizabeth Stack (Robert Stack)

1982: Laura Dern (Bruce Dern, Diane Ladd)

1985: Lisabeth Shatner (William Shatner)

1986: Calista Carradine (David Carradine)

1987: Candace Savalas (Telly Savalas)

1992: Joely Fisher (Eddie Fisher, Connie Stevens)

1994: Alex Martin (Whoopi Goldberg)

1995: Mr. Golden Globe—John Clark Gable (Clark Gable)

1996: Mr. Golden Globe—Freddie Prinze Jr.

1998: Clementine Ford (Cybill Shepherd)

2000: Liza Huber (Susan Lucci)

2001: Katie Flynn (Jane Seymour)

2002: Haley Giraldo (Pat Benatar)

2003: Miss Golden Globe: Dominik García-Lorido
(Andy Garcia) Mr. Golden Globe—A.J. Lamas
(Lorenzo Lamas)

2004: Lily Costner (Kevin Costner)

Bizarre Moments in the History of the Golden Globes

1957—Zsa Zsa Gabor is given a Golden Globe as "the
most glamorous actress" of the year. As the
ceremony drags on, Frank Sinatra and the Rat
Pack hijack the stage to speed things up, and
they're such a hit that they're invited back as
unofficial masters of ceremony the next year.

1971—When Jane Fonda is named Best Actress for
Klute, a Vietnam veteran wearing a tunic with
war medals and blue jeans comes onstage to
accept. The former soldier is booed.

1981—Pia Zadora is named New Star of the Year after
HFPA members are wined and dined by her
husband in Las Vegas.

1993—Rob Reiner tells the *New York Times* there's
something "unkosher" about the Golden
Globes and says, "The main thrust [of HFPA
press conferences] seems to be an elaborate
scheme to have their pictures taken with you."

1996—A *Washington Post* article finds that one HFPA
member only "recently left his job selling
appliances at a Burbank Circuit City."

1999—20th Century–Fox is outraged when only about half of the HFPA's ranks turn out for a screening of *The Thin Red Line*, which is passed over for a Best Picture nomination in favor of the critically reviled *Patch Adams*.

1999—USA Films sends expensive watches from Coach to each HFPA voter on behalf of Sharon Stone, who is subsequently nominated for Best Actress for *The Muse*. When the press gets wind of the story, the voters are told to send back the watches. Stone loses out on the Globe to Janet McTeer of *Tumbleweeds*.

Clichés, Foul-ups and Blunders

On the December 15–16, 2001, edition of *Ebert & Roeper*, we reviewed *Kate & Leopold*, a romantic comedy slated to open the following Friday. Directed by James Mangold, the film starred the end-of-her-perky-phase, pre-wax-lipped Meg Ryan as Kate, a New York market researcher. Her ex-boyfriend Stuart, an oddball science geek played by Liev Schreiber, develops a method of time travel that has him bouncing back and forth between 1876 and the present day. (No frequent flier miles included.) *Kate & Leopold* also starred Hugh Jackman as Leopold, a nineteenth-century nobleman who is Stuart's great-great-grandfather. Stuart travels back in time to observe Leopold from a distance, but on one of his visits, Leopold sees Stuart and chases after him. All hell breaks loose, resulting in Stuart bringing Leopold with him to the year 2001. This leads to the inevitable fish-out-of-water scenes of the perplexed but courtly Leopold strolling Manhattan in his nobleman's outfit as he marvels at laws that require humans to pick up dog poop, tries to figure out how to use a remote control and learns how to use a toaster. And of course he falls in love with Kate. She tries to overcome her cynical nature as she becomes smitten with this seemingly bonkers but utterly sincere gentleman who claims to be from the past. Eventually Stuart comes to realize that Kate herself belongs to the nineteenth century, and that if he doesn't return Leopold and Kate to their rightful place in the time-space continuum, *he* will cease to exist, because, after all, he's Leopold's great-great-grandson, and if Kate and Leopold don't get together in 1876, Stuart will never be born.

Got it?

Of course you're going to have plot-logic problems in a film where characters are hopping from century to century. But I've always loved time-travel movies precisely because they're such inherently preposterous and tremendously giddy flights of imagination, asking us to suspend disbelief and leave behind our acceptance of time's unforgiving, linear nature. Indeed, I recommended *Kate & Leopold*—but I was troubled by one aspect of the storyline that seemed just too weird, even for a time-travel movie. Remember, the Schreiber and Ryan characters had been together for four years before they broke up—but then we learn they're actually related, i.e., she's his great-great-grandma. And in the twenty-first century, they've had sex hundreds of times.

All together now: Ick. Do you really want questions of incest polluting your frothy romantic comedy?

Here's what I said on our show:

Like the *Back to the Future* movies, *Kate & Leopold* involves a folding of the generational space-time continuum that defies logic—but whereas Marty McFly was able to avoid mashing with his mom, Stuart has had a four-year relationship with Kate, which means that if she ends up with Leopold, she'd be Stuart's great-great-grandmother, which is kind of disgusting. But I'm still recommending *Kate & Leopold* for its lovely romance and for the never-ending charm of Meg Ryan . . .

Roger agreed that the situation was unseemly, but he too gave *Kate & Leopold* Thumbs Up.

On December 18, 2001, Miramax announced that *Kate & Leopold* would be pushed back to a Christmas Day release, and that the version seen by critics would not be shown to audiences. The December 21, 2001, edition of *Daily Variety* offered this explanation: "Reviewing pic last week on their syndie review show *At the Movies*, Roger Ebert and Richard Roeper groused that the incest implication left them cold."

Okay, so the show hasn't been called *At the Movies* in a very long time, and it wasn't really a case of both of us "grousing." It was more like I brought it up and Ebert said, "You're right," but whatever.

In a Knight-Ridder article on the postponed release, a Miramax publicity executive said, "We found that what we had originally thought would be an interesting plot point—that Kate and Leopold were Stuart's great-great-grandparents—was being misconstrued to focus on the incestuous situation that relationship would create. That was never the intention of the plot point; we realized people were more aware of those implications than we wanted."

In other words, "Whoops!"

All references to Stuart being a direct descendant of Kate and Leopold were erased from the new version of the movie, which means we lost the incest problem, but we were left with a movie in which Stuart is desperate to transport Leopold back in time for no apparent reason. In a truly ironic move, Mangold also deleted a scene in which a director—played by Mangold—is told by Ryan's market researcher to make changes in his movie because it didn't play well for test audiences. Talk about movies imitating life imitating movies imitating life! Or something.

The DVD of *Kate & Leopold* has a big "Two Thumbs Up!" on the front cover, based on the review we gave of the first version. (Obviously, the second version was released after our program was aired.) You can watch both edits of the film and hear Mangold's comments about the cuts he had to make.

For the record: I like the first version better, even with the unfortunate incest element. In the edited version, where Stuart's very existence doesn't depend on getting Leopold and Kate to travel back in time, his frantic efforts to catapult Leopold back to the nineteenth century are inexplicable.

Of the 1,000-plus movies I've reviewed on *Ebert & Roeper* in the last four years, the *Kate & Leopold* incident is the only time we critiqued something in a film and the problem was addressed in the editing room before it actually hit theaters—but it's certainly not the only instance of a glitch showing up in a movie. In Richard Linklater's invigorating *School of Rock*, there's a scene in which two kids in Jack Black's classroom rock band show up in costumes designed by one of their classmates. The boy is dressed up like the Mini-Me version of the lead singer in Loverboy, and the girl is outfitted in Pat Benatar gear. Black is properly appalled, but he instructs the kids to join their band mates and work on a new song. The scene continues without a break in time—but as the band plays the new tune, the retro-outfitted kids are back in their school uniforms. Obviously the scene in question was filmed in bits and pieces, perhaps over the course of a few days, and a mistake was made.

Think about all the elements that have be in perfect synchronization when a scene is filmed, especially a long and complicated sequence that might take days or even weeks to shoot. Let's say George Clooney and Catherine Zeta-Jones are doing a film noir, and they're shooting a scene that begins with them walking into a crowded tavern and ends with Clooney chasing a suspect out the door. If it's dusk when they enter, it should still be dusk—but just a little bit darker—when the scene ends. If the clock on the wall reads 6:20 when Clooney is talking, it has to be set to 6:20 or 6:21 when Zeta-Jones replies. If Clooney is nearly finished with his beer when he tells a joke, he better not be sipping from a full beer when Zeta-Jones laughs at the joke. The basket of fries on the table shouldn't replenish itself; the condiments shouldn't jump from one side of the table to the next. The extras in the background should be wearing the same outfits and sitting in the same seats; the game on the TV should be progressing in a natural fashion. Let's say there's a giant mirror behind the bar; in that case, we should never catch a reflection of a camera or a boom microphone or a member of the crew.

And that's just the obvious stuff.

There's no such thing as a mistake-free, "perfect" movie. Do a frame-by-frame analysis of any random film and you're almost certain to uncover a gaffe, whether it's a song from 1987 playing in a movie set in 1985, a cigarette changing length in an ashtray or a background extra looking right at the camera or the main characters. Most of these errors are so small we don't even notice them—nor for that matter did the director or editor of the film pick up on it. (Either that or the mistakes were noted too late in the process, and the choice was to lose the scene, or hope audiences and critics wouldn't be troubled by a relatively minor screw-up.) In other cases, though, you have to wonder how the filmmakers could have allowed such a glaring problem to survive the final cut of the film. Glenn Close's suit changing colors from gray to blue to dark brown in *one* courtroom scene in *Jagged Edge*. John Wayne marching toward a sun setting in the east in *The Green Berets*. A clock in *Julius Caesar*. People doing midday activities—kids playing baseball, a mom hanging laundry—as the Japanese attack at dawn in *Pearl Harbor*.

As Jimmy Buffett once sang, math is hard. In the 1984 film *Birdy*, Nicolas Cage and Matthew Modine are in their early twenties in a story set in the early 1970s, but in flashback scenes that occur in the 1950s, they're teenagers. *The Patriot* opens in 1776 and ends in 1783, yet most of Mel Gibson's children are played by the same actors throughout the film, meaning that the kid who looks to be about eleven at the beginning of the story still looks about eleven some six years later. Forget the Revolution, Mel; someone is freezing your kids in time!

As for little Jonathan Lipnicki's assertion in *Jerry Maguire* that "the human head weighs eight pounds," maybe the little whippersnapper isn't as smart as everyone thinks. The human head actually weighs between ten and fifteen pounds, and I don't even want to think about how scientists figured that out.

When they show those blooper reels over the final credits of a film—usually after an unfunny comedy, where they're desperately trying to show us how much fun Jackie Chan or Cammie Diaz or Jerry O'Connell was having on the set—there's often a moment when an actor is called by his or her real name instead of the character's name. An actress says, "Let's go, David!" to David Spade, who's playing a character named Billy, and Spade deadpans, "That's great, but who's David?" and the actress breaks character, and everyone laughs, and we hear the director say "Cut!" and everyone laughs some more—and you turn to your date and say, "Okay, that's enough of that. Can you remember if we parked on level three or level four?"

Sometimes, though, the real-name blunder makes its way into the actual movie.

DAYS OF THUNDER

Tom Cruise plays a racecar driver with a name that sounds like a venereal disease: Cole Trickle. ("According to the AMA, if you're suffering from Cole Trickle, you're going to need a shot of penicillin.") Nicole Kidman is Claire, and Michael Rooker is Rowdy. Cole and Claire visit Rowdy at his house on the lake, and the three of them are taking a walk when Rowdy's wife, Jennie, played by Caroline Williams, joins them.

JENNIE: *"Hi Claire, I'm Jennie. Nice to meet you."*
CLAIRE: *"Hi. Nice to meet you."*
JENNIE: *"Hi Tom."*
COLE: *"Hi Jennie."*

Of course, what Cole *should* have said was, "Who's Tom? I'm Cole, Cole Trickle, racecar driver and free spirit. I don't know this Tom person." Either that or, "Cut! She just called me by my real name!"

Soon after that, Rowdy becomes quite ill. Fortunately, Nicole is playing a doctor.

As for Ms. Williams, the Tom/Cole gaffe, while embarrassing, didn't prevent her from winning roles in *Texas Chainsaw Massacre 2* and *Texas Chainsaw Massacre 3*. She was also Tiny Who Woman in *How the Grinch Stole Christmas*.

SAVE THE LAST DANCE

Sean Patrick Thomas as Derek walks into a restaurant, where his homies are already seated. There's a chorus of greetings along the lines of, "What's up, man!" but then we hear, "What up, Sean," as the camera cuts to Malakai, played by Fredro Starr. Whoops. (You'd think Starr would be particularly sensitive about the whole name thing, given that he has played characters with such monikers as "Go," "Black," "Shorty," "Geronimo," "D-Mack" and "Junior." I'm reasonably sure Humphrey Bogart went his entire career without playing anyone with those names.)

THE DOORS

Val Kilmer plays Jim Morrison and Kathleen Quinlan is Patricia Kenneally, a journalist who introduces Morrison to the world of bizarre rituals, blood drinking, freebasing and nude dancing. Anyway, after *that* courtship, Jim and Patricia are in a backstage shower before a concert. Morrison is freaking out because she has just told him that she did a background check and found out that his parents aren't really dead and he's concocted this whole mythology about himself. In the background, the crowd is chanting for "Jim."

Patricia: "Do you hear them out there? Are you listening to them? It's you they want, Val. It's not the Doors."

See what drinking blood and freebasing wood alcohol will do to a person? You can't even tell your Jims from your Vals!

WAR OF THE ROSES

Oliver Rose (Michael Douglas) is visiting his lawyer friend Gavin D'Amato (Danny DeVito), proudly showing off the blueprints of his house, which has been divided into separate areas for Oliver and his estranged wife, along with some neutral zones.

D'Amato is appalled. He says, "There are other houses! There are other women!"

Oliver responds: "No, no, no, DeVito. I'm going to win, because I've got her to accept the ground rules."

Given the similarities between "DeVito" and "D'Amato," it's easy to see how this mistake could be made. What's not so easy to understand is how somebody on the set that day didn't pick up on it.

In the digital-CGI-DVD era, a film can still be considered a work in progress even after its theatrical run has concluded.

Directors such as Ridley Scott, Peter Jackson, Oliver Stone, James Cameron and Steven Spielberg have tinkered with their movies for theatrical rereleases and for special DVD editions. New footage is added, old scenes trimmed, and creative second thoughts indulged. For example, Spielberg said he had always regretted having the government agents draw their guns when E.T. and his buddies are fleeing the authorities. He corrected this "mistake" by digitally replacing the guns with walkie-talkies for the twentieth anniversary edition of the film and for the DVD.

Anachronisms and technical glitches can also be fixed for DVD releases. On old videotapes of *E.T.*, the family refrigerator changes colors a few times, but on the new DVD, it's an off-white hue throughout the film. In the first *Lord of the Rings*, Frodo and Sam are walking through a farmer's field in Middle Earth when an automobile passes by in the far background, the sun reflecting harshly off its windshield. Alerted to this flub by one of the eight kazillion web sites dedicated to *LOTR*, director Peter Jackson digitally wiped the car from the special edition DVD.

On other films, the foul-ups are still clearly visible.

A PERFECT MURDER

Gwyneth Paltrow is taking a bath, and her hair is in a high ponytail with one of those "scrunchie" deals. After a killer hired by hubby Michael Douglas attacks Gwynnie, the ponytail shakes loose and the scrunchie falls off, and her hair is all over the place. And then: The scrunchie is back! And then it's gone! Ponytail! No ponytail!

CADDYSHACK

Danny (Michael O'Keefe) is meeting with the judge (Ted Knight) in the judge's office, and at one point the judge gets so frustrated with a lamp blocking his view that he knocks the lamp aside and we hear a giant crashing noise. A moment later, the lamp is back on the desk.

FATAL ATTRACTION

It's the morning after Michael Douglas and Glenn Close have slept together. She's in bed and he's getting ready to leave. As they argue, the sheets magically climb up and down Close's torso. One moment, her boobs are exposed. The next, the sheets are up to her chin.

> GLENN: *"You didn't stop for a second to think about me." (Boobs.)*
> MICHAEL: *"That's crazy. You knew the rules, Alex."*
> GLENN: *"What rules?" (No boobs.)*

Then she literally kicks him out of bed! Even though he wasn't eating crackers. And then she slits her wrists.

HOME ALONE

At the beginning of the film, as the family is getting ready to go to Paris, there are a couple of Airport Express buses in front of their house. A redheaded kid in a parka and hat walks over to tell the driver that his family is going to Orlando, but Missouri first. The kid says, "Do you know the McCallisters are going to France? Do you know if it's cold there? Do these vans get good gas mileage?" The driver looks at him and says, "Gee, I don't know kid. Hit the road." And the kid mouths the driver's line, about a half second behind the driver. Then the kid realizes it's his cue, so he turns and leaves.

LETHAL WEAPON

Mel Gibson is on the roof of a building, where his idea of negotiating with a suicide jumper is to handcuff himself to the guy and take a flying leap with him, hoping they'll land safely on the inflatable landing pad. When they're about to take off, you can see that the cuffs are not linked, and when they jump, they hold hands. The cuffs are connected again when they emerge from the landing pad.

MISS CONGENIALITY

In the scene where consultant Michael Caine is teaching would-be contestant Sandra Bullock how to "glide" and they almost get hit by a taxi, you can see an orange fence set up in the background. A ton of "real" people are just standing there, watching them make the movie.

PRETTY WOMAN

Julia Roberts is munching breakfast as she banters with Richard Gere. First she has a croissant in her hand; then it changes to a pancake. Then there's a big cartoony bite in the pancake. Then she takes a second bite. Then we see her holding the pancake and it just has the first cartoony bite. Wow! She's a beautiful hooker with a sunny personality *and* she has a magic pancake! No wonder he falls in love with her.

TERMINATOR 2: JUDGMENT DAY

Sarah Connor, her son John and the Terminator are in the Cyberdyne building when they're confronted by a SWAT team. The commander says, "Okay, drop him!" As they start to fire, you can see somebody who looks like a crewmember walking into the scene, his hands in his pockets.

TOP GUN

Late in the film, long after Maverick's partner Goose has died, there's a flight scene where Maverick's new copilot is supposed to be "Merlin" (played by Tim Robbins), but for a few seconds the guy in the back seat is wearing Goose's helmet. Maybe it's the ghost of Goose! After all, Maverick does say, "Talk to me Goose!" as he looks for spiritual guidance.

WALL STREET

According to the opening title, the movie is set in 1985—but Charlie Sheen's Bud Fox has a conversation with John C. McGinley's Marvin in the office, and Marvin reminds him to call Gordon Gekko. Marvin: "Oh, Gekko, Gekko's beautiful.

Thirty seconds after the *Challenger* blew up, he's on the phone selling NASA stocks short." The *Challenger* blew up on January 28, 1986.

As fun as it is to spot these mistakes, they're minor crimes. The occasional anachronism or even a weird lapse like an actor calling another actor by his real name—these things happen, and it's not going to spoil our enjoyment of the film (if the film is worth enjoying). Nobody's *trying* to screw up, right?

Other cinematic crimes aren't so forgivable. When a star making $10 million a movie can't be bothered with learning a proper accent; when an aging icon insists on casting himself opposite much younger leading ladies; when a director begins a film with that clichéd, sweeping overhead shot of the city, as if we're gliding above the skyscrapers—we're talking about movie felonies.

WOBBLY ACCENTS

Actors love to do accents as much as basketball players love to slam dunk. Nothing says acting like accents! So the Texas-born Renée Zellweger ends up playing Bridget Jones, and Australia native Nicole Kidman plays a Russian in *Birthday Girl*, and the British-born Emma Thompson is cast as the

First Lady in *Primary Colors*. It's a *challenge* for the performer, don't you see? A challenge.

Sometimes it's a challenge for the filmgoer as well. Zellweger's Bridget was a spot-on performance, impressing even the British critics, and Kidman's Russian in *Birthday Girl* was stellar (as was her American accent in *The Human Stain*). But Thompson's Hillary-esque accent, while technically efficient, occasionally delved into caricature. You could see the strain on poor Emma's face as she contorted her vocal mannerisms to sound harsh and midwestern-y.

Then there are the truly wobbly accents, like Angelina Jolie's in the *Tomb Raider* films. At times Jolie seems to forget that Lara Croft is supposed to be British. The great Sean Connery, born in Scotland, doesn't even try to disguise his accent most of the time, whether he's playing an Irish-born cop in *The Untouchables*, a Russian submarine commander in *The Hunt for Red October* or Bond, James Bond.

Some of the more dubious accents in recent years:

Anthony Hopkins (England) as an American professor in *The Human Stain*

Brad Pitt (USA) as an Irish terrorist in *The Devil's Own* and as an Austrian explorer in *Seven Years in Tibet*

Harrison Ford (USA) as a Russian submarine commander in *K-19: The Widowmaker*

Kevin Costner (USA) as the British rogue of legend in *Robin Hood: Prince of Thieves*

Nicolas Cage (USA) as an Italian soldier in *Captain Corelli's Mandolin*

Penélope Cruz (Spain) as a Greek in *Captain Corelli's Mandolin*

Winona Ryder (USA) in *Dracula*

Don Cheadle (USA) as a British explosives expert in *Ocean's 11*

Josh Hartnett (USA) as a British hair stylist in *Blow Dry*

Heather Graham (USA) as an English prostitute in *From Hell*

Keanu Reeves (Canada) as a Brit in *Bram Stoker's Dracula*

Michael Caine (England) as an American adventurer in *Secondhand Lions*

Leonardo DiCaprio (USA) as King Louis XIV in *The Man in the Iron Mask*

ACCENTUATING THE POSITIVE

Anthony LaPaglia has played American cops and toughs in so many movies and TV shows that I was momentarily taken aback by his flawless accent in the 2001 movie *Lantana*, in which LaPaglia played an Australian detective tormented by an extramarital affair. (It's an excellent film. Please rent it.) Then I remembered: LaPaglia is Australian. It's not his accent in *Lantana* that's so impressive—it's his amazing consistency when he plays Americans.

Some other recent examples of great accents:

Judy Davis (Australia) as an American in a number of films, including *Husbands and Wives*

Kenneth Branagh (England) as an American in *Dead Again*

Gwyneth Paltrow (USA) as Brits in several movies, including *Shakespeare in Love* and *Emma*

Nicole Kidman (Australia) as an American in *To Die For* and *Cold Mountain*

Russell Crowe (Australia) as an American in multiple roles, from *L.A. Confidential* to *A Beautiful Mind*

Tim Roth (England) as an American in *Reservoir Dogs*

Gary Oldman (England) as an American in *True Romance*

Cate Blanchett (England) as an Irish journalist in *Veronica Guerin* and an American in *The Gift* and *The Missing*

Bruce Greenwood (Canadian) as JFK in *Thirteen Days*

Meryl Streep in just about everything, though her South African accent in *Out of Africa* has its detractors.

SUBTITLES, PLEASE

I'm the first to acknowledge that Jackie Chan's English is better than my Chinese, but there are times when I'm watching Chan's attempts to speak English in films such as *Rush Hour* and *Shanghai Noon* that I have no idea what he's saying.

This is not a good thing. We like to understand our actors. Some foreign-born stars who occasionally could have benefited from subtitles when doing English-language films:

Jackie Chan
Penélope Cruz
Antonio Banderas
Gérard Depardieu
Arnold Schwarzenegger
Jean-Claude Van Damme

WOODY'S WOMEN

Woody Allen is eleven years older than former real-life love Diane Keaton and ten years older than ex-partner Mia Farrow—but he's at least in the same generational neighborhood as those two fine actresses. There was a certain verisimilitude to the Allen-Keaton dynamic in *Annie Hall*, and the Allen-Farrow relationship in *Husbands and Wives*. But as far back as 1979 and *Manhattan*, Allen's onscreen alter ego was coupling with much younger women. Not until Allen was in his late sixties did he finally relinquish the leading man role in his own movies, handing over the reins to the likes of Jason Biggs in *Anything Else*, thus sparing us the spectacle of a wrinkly little Woody Allen slobbering over a ripe young Christina Ricci.

Age differences between Woody Allen and some of his leading women:

Manhattan (1979)—Allen was 44; Mariel Hemingway was 18.

Mighty Aphrodite (1995)—Allen was 60; Mira Sorvino was 28.

Everyone Says I Love You (1996)—Allen was 61; Julia Roberts was 29.

Small Time Crooks (2000)—Allen was 65; Tracey Ullman was 41.

Curse of the Jade Scorpion (2001)—Allen was 66; Helen Hunt was 38, Elizabeth Berkley was 29 and Charlize Theron was 26.

Hollywood Ending (2002)—Allen was 67; Téa Leoni was 37 and Debra Messing was 34.

SAME OLD SHOTS

Memo to every director in the world: If you're thinking of including any of the following scenes or shots in your next film, please think again.

1. As the film begins and the credits appear, the camera swoops over a large body of water.

2. As the film begins and the credits appear, the camera swoops over a mountain range.

3. As the film begins and the credits appear, the camera swoops over the city.

4. As the film begins and the credits appear, the camera swoops over a lonely stretch of road, where a solo car zips along.

5. On the verge of the most important moment in their lives, a team of cops (jewel thieves, football players, astronauts, whatever) walks in slow motion toward the camera. By God, they're ready.

6. Somebody pulls a gun and makes a threat. The threat isn't taken seriously. The gun-wielder then cocks the trigger to show he *really* means business.

7. After cocking the trigger, the gunman issues a command, which is ignored. The gunman then repeats the command, but this time he shouts—and that always seems to do the trick. ("Take a seat. I said TAKE A SEAT!")

8. Foreshadowing a fatal disease by having a character cough. Once, just once, I'd like to see a follow-up scene where the coughing person says, "Hey, I took some Robitussin and I'm feeling a lot better!"

9. Gunfights where the hero manages to avoid getting shot by poking his head around a doorway— and then pulling back just in the nick of time. Talk about quick reflexes! Of course, when the hero pokes his head out again, the bad guy is reloading, giving our hero time to gun him down.

10. After the big shoot-out in the remote warehouse, the hero limps over to shake hands with his wisecracking sidekick, who has been wounded but is going to be okay. They exchange one last bit of wisecrackery before they share a rare genuine moment of mutual gratitude and respect. They've *learned* from one another. The sidekick is loaded onto the ambulance and the hero gives the doors a strong tap to let the driver know it's time to leave. Next, the hero is reunited with his love interest, who has sustained some artistic, non-facial wounds, and has a blanket draped over her shoulders. As his supervisor approaches and says, "You've got a lot of explaining to do!" the hero flips him off, and he and his lady love leave the scene as the camera pulls back and the jazz score kicks in and we see the flashing lights of dozens of squad cars, ambulances and fire trucks.

Roll credits.

chapter 5

Hype and Whoring

"It doesn't get much better than this."

> —Joel Siegel of *Good Morning America* on the astoundingly awful *The Cat in the Hat*.

"You'll howl with laughter!"

> —Earl Dittman of Wireless Magazine on the jaw-droppingly unfunny *Scooby-Doo*.

"It will scare the pants off you . . . Bring an extra pair!"

> —Joyce Kulhawik of *Hot Ticket*, on the tedious and predictable *Jeepers Creepers 2*.

"Best action, best comedy, best summer movie."

> —Scott Patrick, *Hollywood One-on-One*, on the execrable *Bad Boys 2*, my selection as the worst movie of 2003.

"This is the feel-good chapter of the year! You'll laugh, you'll cry and you'll be on the edge of your seat! Bring an extra pair of pants because the edge of the seat can be sharp! I was born anew and

regained my faith in humanity! Oscar has a new
home and it's Chapter Five!"
—Me.

When *The Matrix: Revolutions* was released in November
2003, Warner Bros. took out full-page advertisements in major newspapers, with a single quote at the top of the ad:

"VISUAL POETRY."
—Richard Roeper, *Ebert & Roeper*

The quote was legitimate, but not entirely accurate.

Normally I'd get a mini-kick out of seeing my name in big
fat letters touting a movie I enjoyed. That's one of the prime
reasons for getting into this business—to impart your opinion to as many people as possible. But there's a big difference
between a critic who is *pleased* when he's quoted and a
"critic" who actually furnishes blurbs to studios or tailors his
reviews in a desperate attempt to be quoted. (And I say "he"
because from what I can tell, approximately 90 percent of all
film critics in the United States are men. I don't know why
that's the case, but I do know that I *don't like this statistic.*)

I did give a qualified Thumbs Up to *The Matrix: Revolutions*, but the "visual poetry" quote is semi-misleading. A little background here. On *Ebert & Roeper*, we review five or
six movies every week, with Roger and me taking turns intro-

ducing the films. The only part of the show that's scripted is that lead-in section, in which the critic says something like, "Our next movie is *The Matrix: Revolutions*, starring Keanu Reeves . . ." etc. After a minute or so of criticism and set-up, the cohost then introduces two or three clips, and concludes with another half-minute of commentary. The other guy is absorbing this for the first time, and once that scripted portion of the review comes to a conclusion, he's free to jump in with spontaneous reaction that includes a vote of Thumbs Up or Thumbs Down. It's been basically the same formula since Siskel & Ebert created the franchise some three decades ago.

As for studios using quotes from the show: Our policy is that anything we say in the scripted introduction/review of the film or in the unrehearsed crosstalk is fair game. Our show is essentially "live to tape," complete with interruptions and pauses and overlapping conversations, and that can make for some blurbs that are somewhat lacking in sophistication and erudition. In the heat of verbal battle or the spontaneity of the moment, I might assess Bill Murray's performance in *Lost in Translation* by saying something like, "Murray's great, he really is, it's really just a terrific performance, he could get an Oscar." That works on the show and I'm fine with it because people talk that way in real life—but it's not exactly how I'd phrase things if I were writing a review. Even though the quotes would be technically accurate, I would cringe at a print blurb that had me proclaiming: "Murray's great! He really is! It's really just a terrific performance! He could get an Oscar!"

Poised at the keyboard, I'd recommend the 2003 version of *The Italian Job* as a breezy, escapist caper film bolstered by slick performances from Edward Norton, Charlize Theron, Mark Walhberg and Jason Statham, who should be cast as the next James Bond. The verbal darts fly as Wahlberg's team of safecrackers matches wits with erstwhile partner Norton, and there's a taut sense of jeopardy in the crime sequences, topped off by some spectacularly implausible chase sequences through the streets of Los Angeles, starring a fleet of Mini Coopers. On the show, as I agreed with Roger's Thumbs Up review, I said, "It's the total package. Just a hell of a ride and we have a great time with it. It's a real marvel of filmmaking. I really, really enjoyed this film." And that's how they blurbed me.

On another occasion, when I concurred with Roger about the Campbell Scott/Hope Davis family-squabble gem titled *The Secret Lives of Dentists*, the ads quoted me as saying, "Big thumbs up. Yeah, brilliantly done." I'm sure that's just what I said, but I'm also sure the "yeah" was used as a conversational comma.

Which brings us to the "visual poetry" of *The Matrix: Revolutions*. In that particular case, I was the lead reviewer of the film and I did write a short review that included that phrase—but I wasn't describing the movie as a whole, I was referring to one specific sequence. Setting up a clip featuring Neo squaring off against Agent Smith for one last epic battle, I said:

Perhaps the most intriguing character inside or outside the Matrix is Hugo Weaving's increasingly powerful Agent Smith, who squares off yet again with Neo in a fight that could determine the survival of humankind.

We showed a snippet of Neo and Agent Smith colliding in a downpour, after which I said,

> There is visual poetry to the rain-soaked duel—but it's no more impressive than earlier battles between Smith and Neo. And that's how I felt about much of *Revolutions*. There's at least one hugely unexpected surprise and it tries to answer some of the mysteries of the Matrix—but it's still the least impressive leg of the trilogy. It doesn't have the cool-cat factor of the first film, and there are no action sequences to rival the freeway chase of *Reloaded*. Nevertheless, big kudos to the Wachowski brothers and the primary acting trio of Keanu Reeves, Carrie-Ann Moss and Laurence Fishburne. They should forever be proud of this three-film epic.

I understand why the studio didn't use anything else from the review, as "It's . . . the least impressive of the trilogy!" is hardly a rave. But the "Visual Poetry" quote is a classic example of some marketing exec presenting a quote out of context to the unsuspecting public.

Not that this happens with much frequency to me. Whether it's Warner Brothers or any of the other studios,

I'm almost always quoted accurately—and when the studio wants to shorten a quote or make minor changes in phrasing or tense, they almost always contact the show for permission. (I'm fine with this as long as the editing process doesn't alter my original intent. If I said something like, "Meg Ryan's performance in *In the Cut* is the prime reason to see this movie. She's absolutely flawless," and they request permission to quote me saying, "Meg Ryan's performance is absolutely flawless," I'll sign off on it.)

Still, those "conversational blurbs" come back to haunt me when a movie comes out on DVD and I'm reminded that I really said that *Swimming Pool* was "wickedly delicious." Apparently I had been possessed by the Lucky Charms leprechaun.

The studios also have the maddening habit of attributing a quote to "Ebert & Roeper," as if we said it unison. For *The Passion of the Christ*, ads said, " 'TWO THUMBS WAY UP! A GREAT EPIC FILM.'—Ebert & Roeper." Well, no. We did give it two thumbs, but it was Ebert who called it "a great epic film," not both of us.

Making things worse, the studios often add exclamation points at the end of each blurb! Like this! So even a measured, somber comment sounds like a dance floor shout-out! It's so silly!

Here are some actual blurbs of mine that for some reason were never used by the studios in their ad campaigns. In the tradition of blurbing, I've added gratuitous exclamation points to every sentence.

The Sweetest Thing—"Proves that a gross-out romantic comedy starring three women and written by a woman can be just as disgusting, degrading and dumb as anything the guys can do!"

Dirty Dancing: Havana Nights—"The story is terribly contrived and the lead actors have no chemistry!"

Half Past Dead—"No, it's not a documentary about Steven Seagal's career!"

Hildago—"This is nothing but a B-movie with better production values!"

Swept Away—"If sharks had circled their raft, I would have rooted for the sharks!"

Ballistic: Ecks vs. Sever—"A loud and stupid non-thriller with the worst title of the year! It's a good thing these two don't get married, because Ecks-Sever sounds like a skin condition!"

Jersey Girl—"Fifteen minutes into the film, Jennifer Lopez dies, and that makes her the lucky one because she doesn't have to see the rest of the movie!"

On the Line—"In this limp-as-a-noodle romantic comedy, Lance Bass is so bland he makes Fabio and Rick Springfield look like Brando and De Niro!"

See Spot Run—"There's a scene in this movie where David Arquette is covered in dog droppings and I thought, 'Well now you know how we feel, pal!' "

Corky Romano—"Chris Kattan is an acquired taste in the same way that chicken pox is an acquired illness!"

The Whole Ten Yards—"There were moments in this movie when I had no idea why everyone was yelling and running and scheming, and even worse, I simply didn't care!"

Welcome to Mooseport—"It's like the pound cake of movies—nice and safe and sweet, but not worth recommending!"

Tomcats—"The women in this movie must be completely lobotomized to fall for these idiots!"

2 Fast 2 Furious—"Cardboard characters exchange limp dialogue before yet another chase sequence that looks like the blueprint for a video game!"

Bringing Down the House—"The white characters are humorless or racist or both, and the blacks are either freewheeling party animals who like to drink and shoot craps—or they're hardcore thugs! Amos and Andy would have loved this movie!"

Charlie's Angels: Full Throttle—"The first *Charlie's Angels* movie was a big, loud, jiggly hit—leading to the inevitable sequel, with Bernie Mac taking over the Bosley role from Bill Murray, who reportedly hated working on that first film! Hey Bill—you oughta try WATCHING this stuff!"

Bad Boys 2—"This is two hours and twenty minutes of explosions, car chases, shootouts . . . the last act is so awful you'd be more entertained if you left, went into the lobby, and contemplated the Junior Mints for a half hour!"

"I hear critics can be bought. From the looks of
them, they can't be very expensive."
—Oscar Wilde

In the summer of 2001, *Newsweek* reporter John Horn
noticed that one David Manning of the *Ridgefield* (Conn.)
Press had given rave reviews to four films released by Sony
Pictures: *Four Feathers*, *The Animal*, *A Knight's Tale* and
Vertical Limit. Heath Ledger of *A Knight's Tale* was "this
year's hottest star!" *The Animal* prompted Manning to say,
"The producing team of *Big Daddy* has produced another
winner!" As for *Hollow Man*, it was "One helluva scary ride!"

The quote for *The Animal* was particularly suspicous, as
the film had not been screened for critics. So *Newsweek* con-
tacted the *Ridgefield Press*, a weekly publication with a circulation of 7,500—only to learn that David Manning did not
exist. Two overzealous executives at Sony had invented Manning and concocted the quotes attributed to him. When the
ruse was uncovered, there was a mighty fuss and holler in the
entertainment industry, with the two Sony executives suspended for thirty days without pay and Sony eventually
agreeing to pay $326,000 to the state of Connecticut for the
deceptive practice. (Later that summer, Sony would get
blasted again when it was revealed the studio had used em-
ployees to tout its own movies in "person on the street" ads.)

And all the while, everyone was asking the same question
about the creation of David Manning: Why bother? Why

bother to invent a butt-kissing, junk-embracing quote whore when there are literally dozens of pseudo-critics and junke-teers on the fringes of journalism who will happily provide quotes to studios or say unbelievably kind things about in-credibly lousy films? As Dennis Miller said about the Man-ning controversy, "Come on, even the real guys aren't real!"

I've said it before and I'll say it again: Virtually every day since I've had this job, someone has approached me and said, "You have the best job in the world! You get to see every single movie!" To which I reply, "Yes, but I also *have* to see every movie." When *Jeepers Creepers 7: Where DID You Get Those Peepers?* rolls around, you'll have the option to laugh at the very idea of wasting 100 minutes of your life on it. I don't have that option. Sometimes as I'm sitting through some excruciating piece of garbage like *The Girl Next Door* or *The Whole Ten Yards* and I'm squirming in my seat and I'm rolling my eyes and the utter pain of it all starts to throb at my temples, I'll be convinced that nobody in the world, not even the director's mother, could possibly find the movie worthwhile, and that every critic from the *New Yorker* to the *Los Angeles Times* to the twelve-year-old writing for www.JustGotMyFirstComputer.com will arrive at the same conclusion. But then the names begin to scroll across my thought process, like credits from hell: Susan Granger. By-ron Allen. Jeff Craig. Mark S. Allen. Shawn Edwards. Bill Bregoli. Clay Smith. Maria Salas. Bonnie Churchill. Sandie Newton.

And of course the immortal Earl Dittman.

These are the names we see attached to the films that almost everybody else hates. These are some of the critics who often get quoted when everybody else is saying, "Run, don't walk, away from this movie!" When the infamous *Gigli* was released on Friday, August 1, 2003, some 275 million Americans found something else to do that weekend, while the critics competed to see who could deliver the most scathing review. Stephen Whitty of the *Newark Star-Ledger* said it was "such an utter wreck of a movie you expect to see it lying on its side somewhere in rural Pennsylvania, with a small gang of engineers circling and a wisp of smoke rising from the caboose." Geoff Pevere of the *Toronto Star* said, "It is an exquisitely bad movie: one to be savored, marveled over, shared with friends and generally appreciated in a state of awestruck wonder." The *Wall Street Journal* named *Gigli* as "The worst movie of the century." On CNN that afternoon, anchor Kyra Phillips told me that the *Atlanta Journal-Constitution* called it "a pile of manure," to which I replied, "Calling it a pile of manure is an insult to manure everywhere." The reaction was so disdainful that Ben Affleck made a game but futile attempt at damage control by going on *The Tonight Show with Jay Leno* and doing a dramatic reading of some of the most scathing criticisms. It seemed as if no one in America had anything kind to say about *Gigli*.

Except a couple of brave junketeers named Allen and Newton, that is. On the film's opening weekend, full-page newspaper ads featured two giant quotes:

"Original with a surprising twist."
—Byron Allen, *Entertainment Studios.com*

"Sexy and fun."
—Sandie Newton, *KTVT-CBS*

Byron Allen is a glad-handing suck-up who does celebrity interviews on a half-hour program that looks like a movie infomercial, with Allen telling the star how wonderful he/she looks, and the star gratefully accepting the praise while strategically positioned in front of a poster for the movie. Sandie Newton has been on such programs as *Hollywood Insider*, and was one of the original hosts on E!, and she is now the entertainment person at the CBS affiliate in Dallas. God bless them, they both apparently enjoyed *Gigli*.

I'm sure all the quote kings and queens are fine humanitarians and hardworking pros who would never compromise their ethics just to curry favor on the junket circuit and impress their bosses by getting quoted in national ads. And from time to time, you could say *I'm* the quote slut, as I've given positive reviews to the likes of *Josie and the Pussycats*, *The Life of David Gale*, *Basic*, *Taking Lives*, *The Butterfly Effect* and *Texas Chainsaw Massacre*, putting me in a distinct minority among critics. (I was right, of course, and the naysayers were all wrong. Ahem.) However, I never furnish quotes in advance of my reviews, and I don't sit on the phone with publicists, trying to come up with the best way to praise a film. (In fact I don't sit on the phone with anyone, as it's just too darned uncomfortable.)

And I can only wish I were as easily entertained as Mark S. Allen of KMAX-TV, who said *Freddy Got Fingered* was "Inspired insanity!"

Or Maria Salas of Telemundo/Gems TV, who proclaimed, *"Battlefield Earth* will rock America!"

Or Susan Granger, who screened the appallingly saccharine and emotionally bankrupt *Dear God* and said the film was "A funny, feel-good 10! You'll have a smile on your face and a tear in your eye at this happy, heart-warming family comedy that's heaven-sent for the holiday season!"

Good Lord.

For years, ads quoting Granger said she was with American Movie Classics—a rather odd credit, given that Granger never actually had a show on AMC, a cable channel that runs older feature films. She did once appear on AMC, and she asked for and received permission to associate herself with the channel. In the late 1990s, Granger began to associate herself with her own web site, SSG Syndicate. (Visit the site and you'll learn that Granger is available for a $3,000 speaking fee, plus travel accommodations.) Granger's reviews usually run about two paragraphs, ending with a rating "on the Granger Movie Gauge of 1 to 10." The dimwitted and cliché-riddled *What a Girl Wants* is a "bright, beguiling, tart 'n' tender 8." The smarmy *Radio* is a "gentle, sweet 7." The dopey and condescending *The Legend of Bagger Vance* is "a spiritual 7." The unspeakably trashy *Charlie's Angels: Full Throttle* is a "fresh, fun-filled, frenetic 7." And the cheesy *Hildago* is "a hard-riding, adventurous 8.

Saddle up for exciting, crowd-pleasing, heart-tugging entertainment."

To be fair, Granger doesn't like everything. Her site contains a number of full-out rip jobs. It's just that when she does
turn in a positive review, it sounds like she's trying out, badly,
for a marketing gig with one of the studios. And at least
Granger cares enough to attend the movies she reviews. The
notorious Jeff Craig of *Sixty Second Preview*, a syndicated radio gig, has publicly admitted he often delegates the actual
watching of movies to members of his staff, because he's just
too busy to attend. Way to respect your profession.

Easily the most famous of the quote sluts is Earl Dittman,
who has become something of a celebrity by sheer virtue of
his head-scratching credit, Wireless Magazine and his seemingly indefatigable zest for terrible movies. According to
CNN.com, Dittman is based in Houston, and Wireless is a
company that includes five obscure publications with titles
such as *Behind the Screen* and *Rhythm and Groove*. My research indicates that he also freelances, with the coveted
Dittman byline turning up in publications in Norway, the
UK and Scotland, as well as the *Sydney*, *Australia*, *Daily
Telegraph* (profiles of actresses Laura Linney and Monica
Bellucci) and the *Perth* (Australia) *Sunday Daily Herald* (an
article on Colin Farrell). Apparently Earl Dittman is big in
Australia. Here's the lead on his profile of Linney: "While

blondes arguably have more fun, the newly brunette Laura Linney proves that being brown doesn't necessarily mean you're bland." All righty then!

Dittman told CNN.com he doesn't supply quotes to the studios, nor does he "critique films. If you want that, look at *Film Comment*. I give people my opinion. Whether everyone agrees or not . . . nobody agrees on [everything]."

One thing that we can agree on: Earl Dittman loves movies. Big movies, small movies, action movies, comedy movies, action/comedy movies, sequels, prequels, trilogies, buddy movies, dramas, romances—if the picture is in focus and the sound is working, you've got a fighting chance of getting an "attaboy!" from the Dittman quote machine. The media are fascinated with Dittman. He's been the subject of a *20/20* segment on ABC and articles in *USA Today* and the *Toronto Star*, and online journalists have skewered him in several in-depth pieces. Dittman was even one of the "critics" named (along with Maria Salas, Jeff Craig and Mark Allen, among others) in a 2001 class-action suit filed by a group called Citizens for Truth in Movie Advertising. They alleged that quote whoring duped them into seeing bad movies and that the studios were essentially purchasing positive reviews by paying all expenses for reporters who come to Los Angeles to screen films and interview the stars. (As of this writing, the suit is still pending; for the record, I think it's ridiculous. If you can't figure out the difference between a big wet kiss from Susan Granger and a rave in *Time* magazine, that's your problem.)

Dittman's more famous than 99 percent of the legitimate

critics in the country—not just because he likes so many movies, but because he likes so many movies that just about everybody else despises. There isn't a critic in the world who doesn't occasionally sound like a gushing schoolgirl with a crush on a pop star—but there's a difference between fawning all over Sean Penn's performance in *Mystic River* and proclaiming that films such as *White Oleander* and *K-19: The Widowmaker* have "Oscar written all over" them.

A partial list of the many mediocre films that have received the Earl Dittman stamp of approval:

Jersey Girl—"Utterly entertaining! Simply irresistible!"

How Stella Got Her Groove Back—"Now that you've exhaled, it's time to groove!"

40 Days and 40 Nights—"A sexy, fresh and wildly hip comedy!"

Drowning Mona—"A comedy classic!"

Against the Ropes—"A true action-packed contender. Gripping and exciting."

The In-Laws (2003 version)—"A knockout action/comedy packed with laughs!"

Boat Trip—"One crazy and daring romantic comedy . . . Vivica A. Fox absolutely sizzles."

Murder by Numbers—"The hottest suspense thriller in town! Bullock is incredible. She gives one of the most astonishingly powerful and fiercely moving performances of her career."

Welcome to Mooseport—"Hilarious!"

Serving Sara—"Matthew Perry and Elizabeth Hurley make an irresistible screen team in this sexy, zany and over-the-top road movie that breaks all the rules. This is one wildly wacky and terrifically twisted comedy!"

Analyze That—"Robert De Niro and Billy Crystal are outrageously hilarious! Their performances are what comedic legends are made of."

Brown Sugar—"[This movie] almost single-handedly redefines the date movie . . . slick, sexy and slammin', like a soulful *When Harry Met Sally* . . . with a hip-hop beat."

A Man Apart—"The film that should turn Vin Diesel into the ultimate hero. A hard-hitting and action-fueled film."

Friday After Next—"The funniest Friday ever!"

How to Lose a Guy in 10 Days—"Kate Hudson and Matthew McConaughey are a match made in movie heaven. Falling in love never looked so exciting."

Scooby-Doo—"You'll howl with laughter."

The Core—"Strap yourself in for the ride of a lifetime."

The Legend of Bagger Vance—"As perfect as any film could get."

Someone Like You—"The most hilarious film of the year."

Duplex—"Hilarious! Smart and wildly funny . . . you'll love this movie!"

One can only imagine what superlatives Dittman would use to laud quality movies. If he believes *Bagger Vance* is "as perfect as any film could get," what would he say about *Mystic River*? But that's just it—we don't know what Dittman thinks of first-rate films because the studios don't need him or Mark S. Allen or Susan Granger or any of the quote champions for those movies. You'll never see a Dittman quote attached to *Memento* or *The Fog of War* or *The Return of the King* because the studios don't need the hacks to pump up the four-star films. They trot out Earl & Co. only after the negative reviews have poured in from the respectable media outlets. If the *Entertainment Weekly* scribe gives your film a D+, is there a three-star review in the *New York Post*? If the *Los Angeles Times* pans your latest release, can you find something quote-worthy in *Glamour* magazine? If the entertainment reporter for a TV station in Chicago doesn't like the film and the junketeer from Boston made a frowny face after the screening in Los Angeles and the hip-hop radio host tells you he just can't recommend your movie—*that's* when you run the quotes from Earl Dittman.

Do the quote whores of the world offend me? Not at all. If anything, I envy them. How fun would life be if you were so easily entertained? "Look honey, it stopped *raining*! That's the feel-good weather development of the week! Wow, that sure was an emotionally involving storm with a surprising twist!"

What's really offensive about the use of cheap quotes is the studio's belief that you, the moviegoer, are stupid. That you don't know the difference between legitimate reviews and cringe-inducing blurbs from quote whores. They're badly misreading the sophistication level of the average moviegoer, who knows full well that if the only quotes you can drum up are from Susan Granger, Jeff Craig and Earl Dittman, your movie is a dud.

Perhaps the most annoying publicity blitz of the young twenty-first century took place in the summer of 2003, when the stars of *Charlie's Angels: Full Throttle* embarked on a worldwide mission to tell the world their movie was all about "empowering women," when in fact it was a cheesy, leering, unfunny action romp featuring three thirtyish women who giggled and jiggled like teenage girls juiced up on too many Red Bulls. Culled from newspaper articles and TV transcripts, here's a list of some of the most pretentious, congratulatory, self-aggrandizing quotes and exchanges to emerge from the *Full Throttle* press tour.

BARRYMORE: *"Each thing leads you to another door. [The plot] is sort of [like]* Alice in Wonderland.*"*

BARRYMORE: *"I like a woman who's feminine but I'm not extremely drawn to girly-girls who are uber-feminine and can't be tomboyish and playful."*

DIAZ: *"I'm half-dude anyhow."*

BARRYMORE: *"You're androgynous."*
DIAZ: *"Very androgynous."*

DIAZ: *"There was a time when my mentality was— (burps loudly). Excuse me. Sorry, I had to."*

BARRYMORE: *"While Charlie is a male figure, what's important is he says, 'I believe in you, you're skilled—and I'm going to give you an opportunity to go out there and save the day, show your capabilities, be heroic, create a family, work together with women in a bonded, family, girlfriend, sisterly sort of fashion.'"*

BARRYMORE: *"[The film] is empowering to women. They have a chance to work together and be heroic, in a sisterly, bonding kind of way."*

DIAZ: *"When we did [the first Charlie's Angels] junket, I think people were thrown off, too, because we were just being organic and genuine to our relationship."*
BARRYMORE: *"Humping each other."*
DIAZ: *"Humping each other."*

BARRYMORE: *"I know what I wanted [the first Angels movie] to be. I love love, and I love couples, and I think about couples going to the movies. I was so*

*profoundly wanting a couple to watch this movie
and have the guy dig what he was seeing—love the
action, love the girls, not bummed out that the girlfriend is dragging him to the movie—yet the woman
[isn't] threatened. The woman is thinking, this is
about women, I am a woman, therefore I can do
this."*

DIAZ: *[while sitting on Barrymore's lap]: "[Drew is]
such a passionate person that I think she's created
this world for herself so she has a place to put that
energy. She has to have a place where she says, 'This
is my passion, this is what I believe in—if you do
not f———follow me on this you're going to be left
behind, because I know.' And she does."*

DIAZ: *"By the way, the two of them [Barrymore and
Liu] are amazing photographers. Unbelievable photographers. Lucy shoots amazing portraits and
Drew shoots the most amazing Polaroids and candid
moments."*

BARRYMORE: *"[Diaz] cooks like a motherf———.
Don't ever eat breakfast without her. Nobody makes
decisions from the heart the way she does."*

What the Hell Happened?

I first became aware of Vin Diesel's potential during a scene from *Boiler Room*, an entertaining junk-bond trader morality tale released in 2000. Standing in front of a giant-screen TV, Diesel was mimicking a scene from *Wall Street*, one of the films aped by *Boiler Room*. (It also plays like a junior college production of *Glengarry Glen Ross*.) With his bouncer's physique, his gleaming pate, his gravel-voiced delivery and his multicultural features, Diesel filled up the screen, dominating his short little white guy costars like Giovanni Ribisi and Scott Caan. Granted, the guy seemed almost uncomfortable reciting his lines, like a linebacker who has to play Stanley Kowalski in the school play to retain his academic eligibility—but he was no worse than Chuck Norris and Arnold Schwarzenegger in their early days (and their middle days, and maybe even their later days), and look at how much fun and money those guys ended up having. Diesel might not have been an actor, but he immediately came across as a *man*. He had presence.

After the movie I did a little research on Diesel's career and learned he had two other mainstream films on his resume. (Three if you count his voice work on *Iron Giant*.) I'd seen *Saving Private Ryan*, but I hadn't immediately realized that the guy from *Boiler Room* was the same guy who had the smallish but important role of Pvt. Adrian Caparzo, a New Yawk motor mouth with an old-fashioned sense of right and wrong. Diesel's other mainstream credit was in the *Alien* knockoff *Pitch Black*, which opened the same weekend as *Boiler Room*. In this so-so action flick, Diesel had the starring role as Riddick, a serial killer with enhanced night vision. When I caught up with *Pitch Black*, I was unimpressed by Diesel's performance. If anything, it seemed like a step back from his work in *Boiler Room*. (Costar Radha Mitchell's assets were more impressive than Diesel's.) My revised opinion was that Diesel might be able to carve out a decent career as an interesting henchman or one of the leads on a TV cop show, but it was evident that carrying a movie—even a second-tier action movie costarring a fabulous babe and a slimy monster—was beyond his capabilities.

He'd have to get better to be as good as Steven Seagal.

One year later, in the summer of 2001, Diesel was anointed as the Next Big Thing in Hollywood when *The Fast and the*

Furious opened with $40 million gross on its way to a domestic take of $144 million. Not that it was supposed to be Diesel's movie. Just as the monosyllabic musclehead Arnold Schwarzenegger had swiped the original *Terminator* from its putative star, the blond and blandly handsome Michael Biehn, the monosyllabic musclehead Vin Diesel stole *The Fast and the Furious* from *its* putative star, the blond and blandly handsome Paul Walker. Even though the cars were the real headliners of the film and Diesel had less screen time than Walker, Diesel was the one getting the magazine covers and the fawning coverage from *Access Hollywood* and *Entertainment Tonight*, and Diesel was the one tapped by the studios as the second coming of Arnold. In a Microwave World where everything has to happen right NOW, the hype machine had knighted Diesel as a superstar without bothering to wait for his career to catch up. *The Fast and the Furious* director Rob Cohen admitted as much in an article in the *Los Angeles Times*, saying, "There's a corporate mentality among multinational companies that we need brand names, whether it's Coke, Pepsi, Nike, Vin Diesel or the Rock. [The industry's attitude is], 'We're not going to wait for them to be stars, we're going to make them stars, demand that the media treat them like stars and we'll pay them like stars, and ultimately, some, in fact, will become stars.'"

Diesel made less than $1 million for *The Fast and the Furious*, but he was able to jack that up to a $2.5 million salary for *El Diablo* (later renamed *A Man Apart*), and he asked for an astonishing $10 million to star in *XXX*, billed as a James

Bond movie for the twenty-first century. Revolution Studios reportedly balked at the $10 million asking price and considered other actors for the lead before caving in to Diesel's demands. After all, Vin Diesel was a superstar, right?

Well, maybe. *XXX*, the insanely hyped action orgy that was supposed to confirm Diesel's mega-star status, had a stellar $44 million opening weekend in August 2002. But there was a huge drop-off at the box office in subsequent weeks, as the reviews were almost universally negative and word-of-mouth was mediocre. Even as an escapist thriller, *XXX* was a disappointment saddled with crummy special effects, a laughable plot and lame dialogue. With a domestic take of $142 million, *XXX* can't be labeled a bomb, but it did fall short of expectations, and it certainly left no footprint on the pop culture landscape.

Also in 2002, Diesel had a supporting role as his usual brooding tough-guy in *Knockaround Guys,* a junior-grade gangster flick featuring characters with self-consciously colorful names like Johnny Marbles and Benny Chains. (It's never a good sign when the screenwriter feels he has to put that much effort into naming the characters.) Costarring John Malkovich, Dennis Hopper and Barry Pepper, *Knockaround Guys* was a slight but effective *Goodfellas* homage, but it sat on the shelf for two years until it was finally released in October of 2002 to capitalize on Diesel's fame. With little fanfare, the film debuted in ninth place for the weekend with a gross of $5 million, earning less per screen than films such as *Brown Sugar*, *Tuck Everlasting* and even *Jonah: A Veggie Tales Movie*. A month later, *Knock-around Guys* was pulled from theaters, having grossed just $11.6 million.

The next "real" Vin Diesel movie to hit theaters was *A Man Apart*, another overblown shoot-'em-up with Diesel playing a rogue cop seeking revenge after his wife is murdered by cutthroat drug dealers, and gee, isn't that an original story! Grossing an underwhelming $11 million on its opening weekend, *A Man Apart* debuted in third place, behind the Joel Schumacher thriller *Phone Booth*, starring Colin Farrell (who was already starting to replace Diesel as the hunk-actor of the moment), and *What a Girl Wants*, a piffle of a romantic adventure for girls not quite sophisticated enough to appreciate the films of Mandy Moore.

The public had spoken, and the public was saying "tween" star Amanda Bynes was the box-office equal of Vin Diesel.

By 2004, Diesel's star had dimmed to the point that the early trailers for the *Pitch Black* sequel, *The Chronicles of Riddick*, featured Dame Judi Dench more prominently than Diesel. The film opened to unspectacular reviews and just OK box office, and did little to advance Diesel's career. In *The Chronicles of Riddick*, Diesel reprises his role as a knife-wielding, goggle-wearing, light-sensitive fugitive and killing machine who gets caught up in an intergalactic battle featuring Necromongers and Furions and Elementals, not to mention Thandie Newton as a scheming temptress who flashes a lot of cleavage. The cleavage gives a better performance than Diesel. In 2005, Diesel will take the title role in *Hannibal*, playing the Carthaginian general who in 300 B.C. mounted an elephant and crossed the Alps to attack Rome. (And if you ever mounted an elephant and crossed the Alps, you'd be in an attacking mood too.) Diesel may yet earn the superstar tag that was handed to him in the summer of 2001—or he could go the way of a dozen other actors who were hyped to the skies before they had delivered the goods. Either way, it would have been nice if the guy had given one memorable lead performance in a top-level film before he was anointed as the Superstar of the Moment.

Some of the most over-hyped "stars" of the last few years:

GRETCHEN MOL

In 1998, Mol appeared on the cover of *Vanity Fair* and had supporting roles in two high-profile films with big stars: *Rounders*, a smart and gritty movie about poker starring Matt Damon and Edward Norton, and *Celebrity*, Woody Allen's wickedly satirical take on Hollywood. Alas, both films tanked, and the next call Mol received from *Vanity Fair* was probably a two-for-one subscription offer. Though Mol went on to do some credible work in films such as *The Shape of Things* and *Sweet and Lowdown*, her resume also includes a slew of movies nobody saw (*New Rose Hotel*, *Bleach*, *Forever Mine*, *Music From Another Room*) and a number of roles in TV movies. Barring an unprecedented career turn-around, Mol's day as a major magazine cover subject are long gone. She's 31—which is like 150 in starlet years.

MATTHEW MCCONAUGHEY

He was supposed to be the next Paul Newman, but he's looking a lot more like the next Sam Elliott—a solid, low-key leading man who will probably graduate to character roles in his forties. In 1996, McConaughey appeared on more magazine covers than just about any established actor, in anticipation of his lead debut opposite Sandra Bullock, Kevin Spacey and Samuel L. Jackson in the John Grisham adaptation, *A Time to Kill*. The reviews were strong and the movie was a hit, but the heat around McConaughey cooled after he starred in a series of big-budget films that performed poorly at the box office and received mixed notices, including *Contact*, *Amistad*, *Ed TV* and *The Newton Boys*. These days McConaughey is doing fine work in little-seen gems such as *Frailty* and playing the amiable romantic lead in commercially successful but artistically uninspired hits such as *The Wedding Planner* and *How to Lose a Guy in 10 Days*. He's doing better than okay, but nobody's comparing him to Paul Newman anymore. In fact, Paul Newman is still doing a better job of being Paul Newman.

PENÉLOPE CRUZ

She's one of the most beautiful actresses in the world and she's a true star in her native Spain, but Cruz has yet to connect with American audiences. (Maybe it's that Topo Gigioon-helium voice.) Ex-boyfriend Tom Cruise is the one who carried the underrated *Vanilla Sky* to its $100 million performance, but Cruz's other English-language films include such critical mediocrities and box-office misfires as *Gothika*, *Masked and Anonymous*, *All the Pretty Horses*, *Blow*, *Waking Up in Reno*, *Captain Corelli's Mandolin* and *The Hi-Lo Country*. (Note: I'm a big fan of the late Ted Demme's *Blow*, which contains an amazing performance from Johnny Depp and good work from Cruz. Please rent it.)

JULIA ORMOND

Amid much fanfare in 1995, Ormond was given the impossible task of living up to Audrey Hepburn's legend in the clunky and utterly unnecessary remake of *Sabrina*. After the film bombed (and deservedly so), Ormond had a starring role in a gripping, intelligent thriller with a horrible title— *Smilla's Sense of Snow*—and then she virtually disappeared from the Hollywood scene. Anybody out there see her in *The Prime Gig* with Vince Vaughan and Ed Harris? The last time I saw Ormond, she was doing a nice job in a secondary role in *Iron-Jawed Angels*, an HBO movie starring Hillary Swank.

SKEET ULRICH

After his star turn in *Scream* in 1996, Ulrich was hailed as the next Johnny Depp. Well, he kinda looks like Depp, but his post-*Scream* filmography includes *Ride with the Devil*, *Kevin of the North* (aka *Chilly Dogs*, and I'll bet you haven't seen it under either title), *The Newton Boys*, *Takedown*, *A Soldier's Sweetheart*, *Soul Assassin* and *Nobody's Baby*. Skeet, we hardly knew ye.

ELIZABETH HURLEY

She's far more famous for her tumultuous romances with cads and millionaires, her TV commercials and her numerous magazine covers than her body of film work, which is highlighted by a sexy comic turn in the first *Austin Powers* movie. Hurley's U.S. bombs include *Serving Sara*, *The Weight of Water*, *Bedazzled*, *My Favorite Martian* and two films with Denis Leary that were never released. (See Chapter 10.)

CHRIS O'DONNELL

After a sparkling turn opposite Al Pacino in *Scent of a Woman* in 1992, O'Donnell was tabbed for stardom, but tepid performances in *Batman & Robin*, *In Love and War*, *The Bachelor* and *Vertical Limit* have pushed him to the back of the line of B-list leading men.

One-Hit Wonders

Each of these actors appeared in one big hit at a young age, but never duplicated that success.

Linda Blair—*The Exorcist*
Zach Galligan—*Gremlins*

Michael Paré—*Eddie and the Cruisers*
Jaye Davidson—*The Crying Game*
Jennifer O'Neill—*Summer of '42*
Michael Biehn—*The Terminator*
Mia Sara—*Ferris Bueller's Day Off*
Jennifer Beals—*Flashdance*

PET PROJECTS

There are times when an actor has a singular vision for a project that seems destined for spectacular failure. When Warren Beatty set out to make a period-piece epic about a communist activist named John Reed, when Kevin Costner drew up the plans for a period-piece epic about a disgruntled soldier turned Indian sympathizer named Dances With Wolves, when Mel Gibson put together a period-piece epic about a Scottish rebel-warlord named William Wallace (not to mention that slightly controversial movie about the last hours of Jesus), the naysayers far outnumbered the cheerleaders. Yet these films became beloved classics. *Braveheart* received ten Academy Award nominations and won five Oscars, including Best Picture. *Dances With Wolves* received twelve Academy Award nominations and won seven Oscars, including Best Picture. *Reds* had twelve Academy Award nominations and three Oscar wins. Beatty, Gibson and Costner each took home the Best Director prize. And *The Passion of the Christ* survived accusations of anti-Semitism and gratuitous violence to become one of the most profitable films ever.

Other times an actor has a singular vision for a project that seems destined for spectacular failure—and the result is even more disastrous than we could have imagined. (Dollar figures have not been adjusted for inflation, as I'm not ranking the films in order of most money lost.)

The Postman (1997)—Costner's follow-up directorial effort to *Dances With Wolves* was a pretentious and unintelligible mythic tale of a heroic mailman. The film cost $80 million and made just $17 million.

Battlefield Earth (2000)—John Travolta tried for years to make a movie based on Scientology founder L. Ron Hubbard's wretched sci-fi novel. *Battlefield Earth* had a budget of $73 million, but looked like an episode of a cheap series on one of those cable channels that rejoices when it gets 200,000 viewers. This ugly, boring and unintentionally funny train wreck grossed $21 million and was on nearly every critic's list of the worst movies of the year.

Hudson Hawk (1991)—Bruce Willis' dreadful caper/comedy combo was budgeted at $65 million and took in $17 million at the box office.

The Razor's Edge (1984)—After *Groundhog Day*, *Rushmore* and *Lost in Translation*, nobody doubts Bill Murray's abilities to take on challenging roles, but twenty years ago, the world wasn't ready for Murray in a stolid adaptation of a Somerset Maugham novel. *The Razor's Edge* made just $6.5 million, and the few people who did see it were laughing in the wrong places.

Mr. Saturday Night (1992)—Billy Crystal's vanity project might have worked as an *SNL* sketch, but neither audiences nor critics warmed to the idea of a feature film about a cranky old comedian.

A number of high-profile actors have signed on for films—but never made it to the final cut, for a variety of reasons.

Eric Stoltz: Spent two weeks filming *Back to the Future* before Michael J. Fox took over the role.

P. Diddy: Was relieved of quarterbacking duties on *Any Given Sunday* by Jamie Foxx.

Lori Petty: Gave way in *Demolition Man* to Sandra Bullock.

Vin Diesel: Left *Reindeer Games* in a dispute with director John Frankenheimer.

Nicole Kidman: Eighteen days into shooting *Panic Room*, Kidman fell and fractured her foot. Producer Jodie Foster stepped in and filming began from scratch—after the sets were rebuilt to adjust for the vast height difference between Kidman and Foster.

Michael Keaton: Woody Allen was deep into the filming of *The Purple Rose of Cairo* when he decided Keaton wasn't right for the lead and replaced him with Jeff Daniels.

Harvey Keitel: His role in *Eyes Wide Shut* was given to Sydney Pollack.

Emily Lloyd: The young British actress worked for a few days on *Cape Fear* before being replaced by Juliette Lewis.

Andie MacDowell: She's seen but not heard in *Greystoke*. Glenn Close dubbed MacDowell's voice.

Ashton Kutcher: Reportedly excused from Cameron Crowe's *Elizabethtown* after script readings did not go well.

John Cusack and Joan Cusack: Left the troubled production of *The Stepford Wives* and were replaced by Matthew Broderick and Bette Midler, respectively.

Principal cast of *September*: Woody Allen killed the first version of his own movie because he wasn't happy with the cast, so he reshot the same film with different actors. Maureen O'Donnell, Christopher Walken and Denholm Elliott were replaced by Elaine Stritch, Sam Waterston and Charles Durning, respectively. (Elliott was given a different role in the second version of the film.)

Cast of *Exorcist: The Beginning*: In November 2002, director Paul Schrader and a cast that included Stellan Skarsgård spent more than three months filming in Morocco and Rome, but studio executives were disappointed in the rough cut. Eventually Schrader was pushed aside and Renny Harlin was brought on to reshoot virtually the entire film, which completed principal photography early in 2004. Skarsgård actually returned to Morocco and Rome to shoot the same role with Harlin (and a new script), but the rest of the original cast was replaced.

chapter 7

Behind the Scenes

October 2003. Publicist and bodyguard in tow, a bearded Russell Crowe enters a tiny, windowless room in the upstairs lobby of the AMC River East Theaters in downtown Chicago, and we're introduced. Crowe is cordial but low-key. Inside the theater, a capacity crowd is watching an advance screening of Crowe's new film *Master and Commander*, after which there will be a Q-and-A session moderated by yours truly.

"I'm going to break the law now if you don't mind," says Crowe as he takes out a pack of cigarettes and a lighter.

The room has white, cinder-block walls, a couple of folding chairs and a card table. It looks like the kind of place where suspects are interrogated. Taped to the wall is a photocopy of a man's driver's license, along with a notice stating that the man is a known sneaker-into-movies. The only other item in the room is a poster for *The Rundown*, an action movie starring the Rock, Christopher Walken and Seann

William Scott. Crowe lights up his smoke, coolly regards the poster and says, "I missed that movie."

"It's actually a lot of fun," I say. "In fact the Rock was here last month and we did a Q-and-A together. He's a great guy. And Christopher Walken has this great scene in the movie where he—"

Crowe stops me short with a quarter-smile and says, "I was being sarcastic, mate."

Oh.

The movie ends and we get the cue to take center stage. As we're making our way to the front of the theater, Crowe says, "Richard, I like to mess around and have a lot of fun with these things. No need for it to be too serious, mate."

"I couldn't agree more. That's the way I like to do these things too, so we'll just wing it and keep it loose."

Once we get started, it's painfully obvious that there are two problems with that plan. First, the audience is mainly composed of members of the Chicago Yacht Club. These are people who own yachts. Average age: about sixty. Last time they stood and cheered for a celebrity: an Elvis concert circa 1970, or never. When I did the Q-and-A with the Rock, the place was rocking with teenagers and twentysomethings who brought down the house when the Rock walked into the theater and put me in a bear hug. This time, when I introduce one of the two or three biggest movie stars in the world, the audience applauds politely.

Problem number two is that the tough-talking, beer-loving, rock-and-roll Russell Crowe is not with us tonight.

Crowe's wife is pregnant, and he hasn't had a drink in more than two months as he trains for his role as the boxer Jim Braddock in *Cinderella Man*. (The clean-living Crowe ended up dislocating his shoulder training for the movie, pushing the release date from December 17, 2004, to March 18, 2005.) The actor wearing Prada shoes and a tailored black suit is in thoughtful, artiste mode. It's not that he's rude or distracted or impatient; quite the contrary. Every question, no matter how innocuous, elicits a lengthy and incredibly detailed answer. Crowe's average response time to any given query is about five minutes. He swears maybe twice, cracks a smile about three times and chuckles politely at my attempts to juice the proceedings. I realize it's time to bring the night to a close when a freelance writer in the audience asks, "Do you believe there are any true Masters and Commanders on the world political stage today?" (For the record: Crowe's answer was, "No, mate.") After we thank the crowd and the spotlights are dimmed and the microphones are turned off, Crowe leans in close, thanks me for the evening and says, "That was a bit fucking deadly, eh?"

What I said: "Well, it's the Chicago Yacht Club. A nice enough group, but after cocktails, dinner and the film, their energy level might not quite be there at ten o'clock at night."

What I was thinking: "Well, I'd like to point out that you were a bit fucking *deliberate* with all your answers, mate. What happened to that whole keep-it-loose thing? Next time guzzle a couple of brewskis and come ready to play, all right?"

This is the thing about an enviable gig. As a great philosopher once said, show me the most beautiful woman in the world and I'll show you a guy who got tired of sleeping with her. Show me someone with the greatest job in the world, and I'll show you someone who occasionally gets tired of it.

In the summer of 2000, when I won the job as the cohost of the most successful movie-review program in television history, I handed my best friend a large polo mallet (Woody Allen reference intended) and said, "If you ever catch me taking this gig for granted or complaining about the workload or taking myself too seriously, I want you to hit me over the head with this, and don't stop until I regain my senses."

Because really. If the worst that happens to you on the job in a given week is that you're not completely satisfied with a personal appearance with Russell Crowe, shut the hell up.

Look at it this way. Let's say there are 10,000 different occupations in the world. The best jobs include gigs like All-Star shortstop for the New York Yankees, billionaire software mogul, and all-powerful ruler of a neutral country of kind and good-looking people. Among the worst jobs: standing on an assembly line in a sweatshop in a third-world country for twelve hours a day while you poke shoelace eyelets into overpriced gym shoes, maid in a seedy motel populated by drug dealers and hookers, and being Rosie O'Donnnell's personal assistant. (Just kidding, Rosie!) If we put Yankees shortstop at No. 1 and sweatshop near-slave at No. 10,000, I'd say that Guy Who Gets Paid Heaps Of Dough to Watch Movies is no lower than No. 20 on the job chart.

Of course, the job is a little more involved than that.

In November 2003, we tackled one of the busiest screening and taping stretches in the history of the show, screening seventeen movies and taping eight shows in a nine-day stretch. Our calendar:

Monday, November 17
10 A.M. *The Cat in the Hat*
12 noon *Bad Santa*
1:45 P.M. *The Barbarian Invasions*

Tuesday, November 18
10 A.M. *The Company*
12:15 P.M. *The Triplets of Belleville*
2 P.M. *Honey*

Wednesday, November 19
Taping two shows

Thursday, November 20
10 A.M. *Love Don't Cost a Thing*
12:30 P.M. *House of Sand and Fog*
3 P.M. *Big Fish*

Friday, November 21
10 A.M. *The Fog of War*
12:15 P.M. *The Statement*
2:30 P.M. *Mona Lisa Smile*

Saturday, November 22
10 A.M. *Cheaper by the Dozen*
12:15 P.M. *Haunted Mansion*

Monday, November 24
Taping three shows

Tuesday, November 25
10 A.M. *Cold Mountain*
12:15 P.M. *Something's Gotta Give*
2:30 P.M. *The Lord of the Rings: The Return of the King*

Wednesday, November 26
Taping three shows
We also screened the six-hour HBO miniseries *Angels in America* on home DVD.

TOP TEN QUESTIONS PEOPLE ASK ME ABOUT MY JOB

Q. How many movies do you see every week?

A. On *Ebert & Roeper*, we review an average of five movies per show, though it can be as few as four and as many as eight. We also do one or two video picks. Our screening schedule also varies, but in a given week, we see more films than we ever discuss on the show. We're almost always going to review the big films opening in 3,000 screens across the country, but we also feature movies opening only in New York and/or L.A., independent and foreign films, documentaries and films making their debuts on HBO, Showtime or other cable networks. The key word we use in evaluating these films is whether they're "reviewable," i.e., is it something of interest to the viewers, something that deserves a wider audience, something that might spark an interesting debate between the cohosts? There's no point in spotlighting a little-known independent feature starring a cast of unknowns that's playing in only one market if we're just going to dump on it.

But there's just one method of determining if a movie is reviewable: You have to watch it. Often I'll screen a film that never gets onto the show. So—we review an average of five movies per week on the show, but I see an average of six movies per week, every week, for a total of approximately 300 films per year.

Q. Where and when do you watch the movies?

A. Most of the films are shown in a private screening room in downtown Chicago that seats about fifty. Sometimes it's just Roger and me and someone from our staff; at other times, the room is packed with other critics and entertainment reporters from the Chicago area. There's no concession stand, but we're allowed to bring in coffee and food.

Screening-room movies usually show at 10 A.M., 12:15 P.M. and 2:30 P.M., with just enough time between films to stretch a bit or run out for coffee. We never see commercials or trailers before the movies, *thank God*.

About once a week, I'll attend an evening screening in a commercial theater, which is usually packed with people who have won tickets from one of the local radio stations or newspapers. Sometimes the studio insists we see a film with an audience (usually the film is a comedy or a slasher flick), presumably because they believe we'll somehow be influenced if "regular people" find the movie hilarious or scary. I can honestly say that crowd reaction has no bearing on my opinion, other than the times when I've wondered, "What in the *world* are these people laughing at? Are they all on drugs?"

Each year I also screen a handful of films on studio lots in Los Angeles, and I see a total of about twenty movies every year at the Sundance and Toronto Film Festivals.

Q. You don't get to watch the movies at home?

A. Even before concerns about piracy, the studios almost never sent out VHS or DVD copies of big-budget films such as *The Aviator* or *Finding Nemo* until the end of the calendar year, at awards-voting time. They want you to experience the movie in a theater environment, and justly so. However, I do occasionally screen documentaries and smaller films at home. In many cases the filmmakers are all too happy to furnish me with a home copy in the hopes that the film will be showcased on the program. In fact, I first saw a little independent feature titled *My Big Fat Greek Wedding* on tape, and later screened it at a theater.

Q. When and where do you tape your show?

A. The show has always taped in Chicago. When I joined the program, we were taping in the CBS studio where the Nixon-Kennedy debate was held in 1960. Now we're at the ABC affiliate in Chicago, on the same hallowed ground where Oprah used to do her program before she built her own studio. From time to time I'll hear from people who swear they've been in "the theater" where we tape our show, but it's a set.

Q. Have you ever walked out of a movie?

A. Never. I feel it's my responsibility to stay until the bitter end of even the worst junk such as *Swept Away* and *Bad Boys 2*, if only to stack up the arguments why you shouldn't waste your time and money on these movies.

Q. What if you have to go to the bathroom during a movie?

A. I rarely take a bathroom break during a film—but the men's room outside our screening room actually has the sound piped in, I kid you not. Of course, this isn't much help if we're screening an Iranian documentary. (Our screening room is on the sixteenth floor of an office building, and the office for a local health club is just down the hall. Imagine if you're visiting the health club office, and you have no idea that there's a miniature movie theater on that floor, and you excuse yourself to use the men's room—and while you're in there doing your business, you begin to hear dialogue from a movie. Also, there is a Jane Fonda sticker at the bottom of the urinal in the men's room. I don't know who put it there, but I hope he was wearing surgical gloves when he was making his little political statement.)

Q. Do you and Roger Ebert ever talk about movies in the screening room?

A. We talk only about films we've already reviewed on the show. If we haven't yet done a film, we don't talk about it off-camera.

Q. Is the show scripted?

A. We begin each review with one of the cohosts reading a short, scripted commentary that sets up the plot and two or three clips. The crosstalk that ensues is unrehearsed and spontaneous. (On occasion we will re-tape a crosstalk if there's a technical problem, a factual error or some other snafu. But we try to avoid it at all costs. The show is essentially taped in "real time.") Neither of us knows what the other thinks of a film until that moment.

Q. Have you ever changed your mind about a review?

A. Sometimes I'll be flipping channels and I'll come across a movie I recommended, and I'll have a hard time remembering *why* I gave it a Thumbs Up. A recent example would be *Legally Blonde 2: Red, White and Blonde*, a cookie-cutter, dumbed-down sequel to the original charmer. I gave it a very qualified recommendation, primarily on the strength of Reese Witherspoon's breezy performance as the cheerful-to-the-point-of-near-insanity Elle Woods—but I can go the rest of my life without seeing *Legally Blonde 2* again. If you haven't seen it, you can still sleep well tonight.

On the flip side, I've had second thoughts about Thumbs Down verdicts on a handful of films that have captured my attention either on cable or DVD. That group includes *Joy Ride*, *Lovely & Amazing*, *Pirates of the Caribbean*, *Gothika*, *I Capture the Castle*, *A Song for Martin* and *The Pledge*. I'm not reversing my position on these films—but there are levels of Thumbs Up and Thumbs Down. Sometimes I give a film Thumbs Up; sometimes it's Thumbs Way Up, or, a Big Thumbs Up, or my personal favorite, an Enthusiastic Thumbs Up. Conversely, there is a difference between a Thumbs Down for *Tomcats* and a Thumbs Down for *Hellboy*. On a five-star rating system, I'd give *Tomcats* zero stars, but *Hellboy* would get two-and-a-half stars.

Q. Do stars or directors ever confront you about negative reviews?

A. Occasionally. We were booked to be on *The Tonight Show* with Ben Stiller, who was still steaming over a double Thumbs Down for *Zoolander*. In Leno's guest book, Stiller suggested that we take our two thumbs and shove them. I declined the suggestion, though I'd rather do that than sit through *Zoolander* again.

The Five Dopiest Questions People Ask Me about My Job

1. Do you really have to see all those movies?

2. Do you see the movies before they're in theaters?

3. Do the studios pay you to give good reviews to their movies?

4. Are all those arguments on your show for real, or do you disagree on purpose so it'll be more interesting?

5. Can I have free movie tickets? You have free tickets to all the movies, right?

Excerpted from reports I filed for the *Chicago Sun-Times* and the New York Times Syndicate, here are some first-person highlights from my adventures at the Sundance and Toronto Film Festivals, and the Academy Awards:

SUNDANCE FILM FESTIVAL, JANUARY 2001

Courtney Love is splayed out on a futon in a sparsely populated room on the second floor of a mansion in the hills, tucked away from the pulsating madness of the party below. Her hair is white blond and one leg is over here and one leg is over there, and she is swigging from her own personal BYOB bottle of booze, and the net effect is that she's just like an actress playing Courtney Love in the movie that will undoubtedly be made one day about the life and times of Courtney Love.

I'm also in that room on the second floor, leaning over the railing and watching the action below. Two DJs imported from New York are spinning vinyl for about

200 dancers. Many of the young women (actresses) look like Piper Perabo and Amanda Peet; many of the men (director/writers) have that carefully constructed, studiously messy hair, and big chunky glasses. Among the dancers is David Alan Grier, who looks as if he's doing a skit from his old *In Living Color* show: "Dancing with White People!"

The party is at the zillion-dollar Hugo Boss house, which has been rented for the night and transformed into a club, complete with headset-wearing door-persons, fully staffed and stocked bars and a magic room where certain partygoers are handed genuine Hugo Boss white jackets. As I was walking in, actress Amy "Road Trip" Smart was walking out, door prize slung over her shoulder.

Time to go to the movies. I expected to spend a lot of time on Main Street, which still has that old mining town feel. But there's only one theater there, the Egyptian, which means festivalgoers spend a lot of time riding shuttles to such glamorous venues as the Park City Library and makeshift theaters in hotel banquet rooms.

Every screening is packed. In fact, there's a long line of standby hopefuls outside most venues, along with ski-jacketed folks walking around saying, "Anybody selling? Who's got two?" as if they were outside a sports arena at a playoff game.

A dark comedy called *Nobody's Baby* premieres at the Eccles Arena, and most of the cast is in attendance—Gary Oldman, Mary Steenburgen (with untoupeed husband Ted Danson), the gorgeous Radha Mitchell. I'm sitting just behind Oldman, and it's weird to watch somebody watching himself on a giant movie screen. (Especially in a situation like this, as the running joke in the movie involves Oldman's persistent itch in a very intimate area.) Oldman also imitates a coyote in the movie. After the screening, the director and cast assemble onstage for a Q-and-A, and somebody in the audience, perhaps having lost a bet, asks Oldman to imitate a chicken. And so one of the most respected actors of his generation obliges, sticking his hands under his armpits and clucking madly while bobbing his head.

Good chicken.

A party at a private residence, and I'm trying to get to the bathroom, but to do so I have to navigate past Stephen Baldwin, who's in a cowboy hat, cowboy boots and a race car driver's outfit, dancing madly by himself near the speakers. He takes off his jacket and sweater, revealing far too many tattoos.

Despite the presence of all these rock gods and movie stars and temperamental artists and supermodels, reports of debauchery and misconduct are sparse. The two best stories: Comic genius Denis Leary was at the Riverhorse Cafe with his *Double Whammy* co-star

Elizabeth Hurley, and Leary got into a tussle with a waiter who wouldn't serve him a drink. Turns out the supposed waiter was actually a busboy who couldn't legally serve alcohol, and a contrite Leary reportedly returned to the bar the next night.

Meanwhile, the famously bratty Hilton sisters—Paris, 19, and Nicky, who's all of 16—have been ripping up the town, drinking vodka and dancing onstage and knocking over drinks and furniture and knickknacks at VIP events and private parties. Well-bred, girls. Well-bred.

The Sundance awards are low-key and just this side of cheesy, given that the venue is the Park City Racquet Club, which resembles a high school auditorium with really crummy plastic folding chairs. Host Donal Logue sets the tone with his jeans-and-oversized-shirt ensemble, his genuine enthusiasm and his wry asides. After the brisk awards ceremony, there's a gargantuan party with lots of dancing and drinking and eating and last minute schmoozing. Actress/filmmaker Joan Chen and supermodel James King are the visual standouts. Past midnight, I hop on a mini-shuttle along with the featured players from *Southern Comfort* (a documentary about transgendered friends living in the Deep South), including the statuesque "Lola Cola," who would tower over Stephen Baldwin even if Baldwin were standing on Eric Stoltz's shoulders. One member of the entourage sits next to me, and we have a pleasant conversation. At one point she says conspiratorially, "There's talk of everyone hitting the hot tub at the hotel."

There's research and there's research. I bid a friendly farewell and hop off at the next stop.

Dissolve back now to the scene of Ms. Love at the party, getting to her feet at 3 A.M. and hugging everyone as she makes her way downstairs and into the night. A few minutes later, I track down the friends who have given me a ride to this party, and I persuade them to leave, with this irrefutable point: If you're at a party and Courtney Love has called it a night, you've stayed too long.

ACADEMY AWARDS, MARCH 2002

LOS ANGELES—Sting is facing a chattery crowd of several hundred actors and producers and agents and studio executives at the Mondrian Hotel, and he is having trouble getting everyone's attention.

"This is a very tough room," he says. "Maybe if the person next to you is still talking, you can tap them on the shoulder and say, 'Sting is going to do a song now.' Thanks."

With that, Sting begins playing his Academy Award–nominated "Until"—but he never quite captures the room.

Only at a Hollywood party would you see so many people who can't shut up long enough to hear a legend perform.

SUNDANCE FILM FESTIVAL, JANUARY 2003

PARK CITY, UTAH—It began with Oscar winner Al Pacino and ended with Oscar winner Anna Paquin, and in between there were 10 movies, nine parties, 27 cups of coffee, 18 shuttle bus rides and two J.Lo sightings.

FRIDAY. Prior to a screening of *People I Know*, there's a small party for about 25 people. Al Pacino hasn't had a chance to see a lot of Oscar contenders, so he asks me what's good and I give him some recommendations. We also talk for a while about what makes a movie resonate.

"For me, I know it's a good film when I find myself thinking about it days later," says Pacino. "But to really appreciate a film, it takes time. You have to step away . . . give it a chance to breathe."

As for *People I Know*, Pacino says, "It's hard to get a handle on it, especially the first 15 minutes. I'm trying to come up with the one thing to describe it, but that's *your* job, isn't it?"

Cue the waiter, who as Pacino finishes an appetizer, says, "I'll take your skewer for you."

I noted that I've never heard a man say that to another man.

"Maybe that's the catch-phrase [for the movie]," says Pacino. " 'I'll take your skewer for you.' "

SATURDAY. At the Park City Library, a packed house gasps and applauds for *thirteen*, starring Evan Rachel Wood as a seventh-grader who spins out of control in a drug-fueled medley of shoplifting, purse-snatching, tattooing, body- and tongue-piercing and casual sex. Little wonder that she forgets to turn in her science project on time.

The most jarring thing about *thirteen* is that it was co-written by Nikki Reed, who co-stars in the film as Wood's deeply troubled and wildly promiscuous best friend. Reed was all of 13 when she co-wrote the screenplay, which is depressing if you're a twentysomething aspiring screenwriter—and frightening if you're the parent of a young girl.

SUNDAY. After many of these screenings, there's a Q-and-A with the stars. It's amusing as hell to see the likes of Dustin Hoffman, Salma Hayek, Andy Garcia, Holly Hunter, Peter Fonda, Alec Baldwin and Penélope Cruz on stages of high school auditoriums or a small town library, tackling questions that range from, "How did you pick this project?" to "What was it like working with [fill in the name of the co-star]?" to, "Why did you pick this project?"

MONDAY. At a tent party for the Eddie Griffin movie *Dysfunktional Family*, I'm introduced to Anna

Paquin, who won Best Supporting Actress when she was just 11 for *The Piano* and has appeared in such films as *X-Men*, *Almost Famous* and *25th Hour*. She's here in support of *Buffalo Soldiers*, a *M°A°S°H*-like military comedy. Only after Paquin begins chatting about the *Lord of the Rings* films and what they did for her country's economy do I remember that she grew up in New Zealand. Having just arrived in town, she asks me what she's missed, and I get her up to date on movies and feed her some slightly mean celebrity gossip. Paquin says, "Meow!"

ACADEMY AWARDS, MARCH 2003

Clutching his freshly minted Oscar backstage Sunday night, Adrien Brody told reporters he had no regrets about mashing with a startled Halle Berry onstage.

"Well, if you ever have an excuse to do something like that, that's it, so I took my shot," said Brody, who added that Berry kissed him back.

Of course, she would have been within her rights to push him away and slap him good. Now THAT would have been an Oscar highlight.

It would have been interesting if Berry's husband, singer Eric Benet, had run into Brody at one of the post-Oscar parties. Would he have cracked him across the jaw, or said, "Congratulations on the Oscar AND tickling my wife's tonsils!"

Reports indicate that Benet seemed almost dazed

by events but didn't want to comment. I'd wonder, though: Would America have been so charmed by the moment if a virile young black actor in his 20s had leapt to the stage and stolen a mouth-to-mouth kiss with someone like Reese Witherspoon while her husband looked on from the audience?

It sounds like a scene out of *Sweet Smell of Success* or an old Jimmy Cagney movie: At the *Vanity Fair* party, mega-agent Ed Limato approached a *New York Post* columnist who had written an item alleging that a number of A-list stars had planned to boycott Limato's annual Oscar party because Limato client Mel Gibson is making a controversial movie about Jesus that reportedly places the blame for Christ's death on the Jews.

"Are you Richard Johnson?" asked Limato. When Johnson said yes, Limato tossed his martini at Johnson, bouncing a couple of olives off Johnson's face and soaking his shirt.

"Do you want to do something about that?" Limato reportedly said, but Johnson declined to put up his dukes.

A classy, peacenik move. But wouldn't it have been great if Johnson had said, "Let's take it outside!" and hundreds of the biggest names in Hollywood had followed them onto the street? Imagine Sheryl Crow, Natalie Portman, Colin Farrell, Ben and J. Lo, Kate Hudson, Nicole Kidman, Bono and Keanu Reeves all chanting

"Fight, Fight, Fight, FIGHT!" as the superagent and the powerful gossip columnist punched each other out until some couple like Susan Sarandon and Tim Robbins jumped in to say, "Break it up, break it up!"

Then again, maybe the peace-sign-flashing Robbins wouldn't be the first one to call for a nonviolent resolution after all. Another gossip columnist, Lloyd Grove of the *Washington Post*, reports that he had a chilling moment after Robbins determined that Grove had interviewed Sarandon's conservative Republican mother, a staunch supporter of President Bush.

According to Grove, Robbins "moved within inches and said into my ear: 'If you ever write about my family again, I will [bleeping] find you and I will [bleeping] hurt you.'"

My Lord! I like to think of Robbins as *The Shawshank Redemption*'s Andy Dufresne, but that's very *Arlington Road* of him.

In the interest of love, I have to report that not all the coupling at the Vanity Fair party was of the confrontational variety. Ben and J-Ben were spotted making out on a sofa, Bono's wife sat on his lap and oldsters Farrah Fawcett and Ryan O'Neal were partying together like it was 1989.

SUNDANCE FILM FESTIVAL, JANUARY 2004

PARK CITY, UTAH—And they wonder why Sundance has a reputation for showcasing dark films: In one day, I saw two features—*Garden State* and *Employee of the Month*—that featured a sidekick character who works with dead bodies (one's a gravedigger, the other is a coroner) and regularly steals jewelry from corpses. And in both films, we're supposed to like these guys.

Apparently under the impression that actors with films at Sundance are supposed to dress up as the Sundance Kid, Ashton Kutcher showed up at the premiere of *The Butterfly Effect* in a Marlboro Man coat, a cowboy hat and a 1970s mustache. He looked like he was auditioning for a Village People tribute group.

"Do You Have Any Idea Who I Am?"—Message on the front of the T-shirts worn by all staffers at the Morning Ray Cafe at the top of Main Street. "Good. Then We're Even."—Message on the back of the shirts.

Sight seen outside the Skyy Vodka Lounge: two women wearing pink hats emblazoned with the words "VAGINA WARRIOR." They're promoting *Until the Violence Stops*, a documentary about Eve "The Vagina Monologues" Ensler and her "V-Day" movement against violence toward women. The V-Day protests take place on Valentine's Day, and this year more than 1,000 cities are scheduled to host activities.

Applause for anything that adds some substance to the stupid-fake "holiday" of Feb. 14—but those hats! It takes a certain kind of confidence to walk around in broad daylight with "VAGINA WARRIOR" on your head.

On the shuttle buses, at press headquarters, at the parties, in the coffee shops, on the street, you get the same question: "What have you seen so far?"

For amusement purposes only, I started throwing out titles of fake movies from *Seinfeld* episodes: "I loved 'Prognosis Negative' and I thought 'Rochelle Rochelle' was just amazing, but I wasn't such a fan of 'Death Blow.' And whatever you do, avoid 'Brown-Eyed Girl.' " Most Sundancers caught on, but a few are probably still trying to track down screenings of "The Muted Heart" and "Chunnel."

ACADEMY AWARDS, FEBRUARY 2004

Donald Trump is right *there* and Paris Hilton is over *there*, just yards away, and they're moving toward each other. Now if I can just get her to muss up his hair as I capture it on videotape, we're talking about an eBay grand slam.

The combed-over, reality-TV mogul and the platinum-haired, reality-TV bimbo were among the celebrity crowd mixing it up at 1 A.M. Monday at the *Vanity Fair* bash at Morton's, traditionally the most star-studded of the Oscar parties—and the finish line for your correspondent's annual Academy Awards journal.

FRIDAY: The 41st annual Publicists' Guild Luncheon is held at the Beverly Hilton, in the same ballroom where they hold the Golden Globes—but instead of TV and movie stars, the room is filled with the people who represent TV and movie stars. So, cell phones chirp like annoying sparrows, as many publicists do not believe in the "Silence/Vibrate" mode. (Personally, I think the only way to vibrate is in silence, but that's because of my Catholic upbringing.)

Host Jimmy Kimmel says, "You people need a publicist for the publicists' luncheon, because I've never heard of it."

As Kimmel introduces guests and honorees ranging from Kiefer Sutherland to Julie Andrews to Marcia Gay Harden, the recurring theme is that none of these people will do his show. After the marketing team for *Pirates of the Caribbean* is honored, and the chief publicist says Johnny Depp and the rest of the cast "did everything we asked them to do," Kimmel says, "Except my show, and I'm reasonably sure we asked them to come on. . . . [If you can get Depp], we can bump the neighbor from *According to Jim*."

Accepting his lifetime achievement award, Clint

Eastwood thanks his publicists but notes, "You never got me on Jimmy Kimmel's show."

SATURDAY: The Independent Spirit Awards are held each year in the middle of the day on the beach in Santa Monica, under a gigantic tent. By 11:30 A.M., the bar is open and the stars are milling around under the tent and outside near the upscale port-a-bathrooms, which feature some genuine fake marble sinks, and a fine collection of colognes and mouthwashes.

Lost in Translation is the big winner of the day, with Sofia Coppola and Bill Murray among those taking home the Indy. Or is it the Spirit?

Everybody loves the Spirit Awards because they're so casual and laid-back. You can tell that these stars spent a lot of time perfecting a look that says, "I didn't spend any time getting ready."

Per tradition, some brave actors perform lame-ass musical numbers spoofing the films nominated for the ISAs' best feature award. Michael McKean and Erika Christensen spoof *Lost in Translation* with their version of "I Am 16, Going on 17," with Christensen singing, "I am 23 going on 24," and McKean responding with, "I am 53, going on 54 . . ."

We also get Juliette Lewis saluting *Raising Victor Vargas* with a custom-cut version of Robert Palmer's "Bad Case of Loving You," and it sounds worse than it reads.

Later, presenter Tom Cruise tells the crowd, "When I was a kid, every newspaper I delivered, every grass I mowed . . . was leading to this . . . I love movies."

Controversial stance. He *loves* movies! Who knew? If only Cruise had turned his speech into a musical number, set to the tune of "Every Breath You Take." *Every grass I mowed . . .*

After the show, the attendees head to their limos as they tote their leather goodie bags filled with such In-dependent-ly Spirit-ed products as Starbucks coffee, Turning Leaf wine, Kiehl's hair-care products and cer-tificates for three nights at a resort in the Dominican Republic.

Oh, and a complimentary eyebrow-shaping. Be-cause of course, nothing says indie film like a finely tuned pair of eyebrows.

SUNDAY: The Bleacher Creatures are in place hours before the first arrival, and they cheer wildly at the sight of anything approaching a celebrity, including the ghastly mother-daughter combo of Joan and Melissa Rivers, who will spend the next few hours on the E! Channel, offering their unique brand of offensively clueless commentary.

Everywhere you turn, TV people are talking about fashion. Let me just say this for the record: I don't care "who" anyone is wearing. And if I hear one more middle-aged white person say "bling-bling," I'm going to start a campaign for a constitutional amendment to permanently ban the word.

More than two hours before the start of the show, attention-junkie and former nominee Sally Kirkland arrives and works the press line as if her life depended on it. Reporters and photographers take this as an opportunity to make sure their microphones and cameras are working.

Rumor has it that later this same evening, Kirkland will be showing up at the opening of an envelope.

Cleavage is in this year, in a big way. Susan Sarandon, Jamie Lee Curtis, Nicole Kidman, Angelina Jolie and Julia Roberts are among those choosing to go deep with the necklines. This is so much better than Bjork dressing like a bird.

After the traditional traffic jam on the red carpet, with all the big stars waiting until the last possible moment to show up, and the announcer frantically asking everyone to take their seats, the show begins with Billy Crystal doing the usual routines. Later in the broadcast, the original musical number by Jack Black and Will Ferrell, "You're Boring," set to the tune of the orchestra music that kicks in when an acceptance speech runneth over, is hilarious:

———

This is it, your time is through
You're boring
You're rambling on, no end in sight
You're boring
No need to thank your parakeet
You're boring
Look at Catherine Zeta-Jones, she's snoring

———

Great stuff. Why not bring those guys back next year to host the whole thing?

Backstage with the press, supporting actor winner Tim Robbins says, "All I can say is register to vote, get involved in the process. . . . I do think that someone has to ensure that the elections are fair. I'm really nervous about computerized elections . . . for the first time in our democracy, we can't have a recount, so that's something people should look at."

In the meantime, *The Lord of the Rings: The Return of the King* keeps winning award after award after award. I'm going to have to see this movie, as it seems to be quite popular.

After the most predictable Oscars in anyone's memory, it's off to the parties, with a quick stop by the *InStyle* bash to confirm that Prince is indeed smaller than the smallest Hobbit, before I join the crowd at the *Vanity Fair* party, which is so exclusive that even people holding shiny new trophies, and actors such as Sir Ian

McKellen, are forced to wait outside and go through a battery of security checks before gaining admittance.

The *Vanity Fair* party is like a wedding reception, except every other face is famous. You've got the big tent, the open bar, the 1980s dance tunes, and the clusters of partygoers all dressed in their best clothes as they hoist drinks, hug one another and try to make themselves heard above the din. You got your Tim Robbins, your Susan Sarandon, your Amy Smart, your Catherine Zeta-Jones, your Renee Zellweger, your Mischa Barton, your *Queer Eye* guys, your Billy Baldwin, your Jude Law, your Joni Mitchell, your Patrick Swayze, your Christian Slater, your skinny supermodels, your *Sex and the City* cast members, your Paris Hilton, your Donald Trump.

Smoke dominates the room. They actually have free, individual cigarettes available in tumblers set out on the bar, and it feels like only about seven people aren't partaking. The net effect is that the most glamorous party of the Oscar season is smokier than the Billy Goat Tavern in Chicago on a Friday night.

And there ain't a cheeseburger in sight.

Let's Go to the Movies

I'm often asked if I feel bad about ripping a movie to shreds on national television. Hundreds of people, from the director to the actors to the crew, have expended great amounts of time and effort and creative energy to make the best film possible. Teams of writers work on a screenplay for years, a producer begs and pleads with the studio for funding, a director dedicates mind and heart and soul to mapping out the story, the cast and crew spend months working together— and then I dismiss the movie with a downward thumb and a three-minute rant. Isn't that unfair?

No, and I'll tell you why. I sincerely appreciate how long and arduous the moviemaking process can be, and I believe that just about everyone in the industry—even the easily-criticized, profit-obsessed studio heads—wants to make good films that entertain and sometimes enlighten and enrich us. Hey, I want them to make good films too. I don't walk into the screening room thinking, "Sure hope this film is a pretentious mess!" But my obligation is not with the film-makers, but with the filmgoers—the viewers who watch our show to figure out which movie to attend. I don't feel bad about telling the audience why I think a film didn't work, but I *would* feel bad if I weren't completely honest in warning people away from a mediocrity. You work hard for your money, and I don't want you blowing it on *Marci X*.

The moviegoing experience is increasingly costly and time-consuming. Your investment goes beyond the $8 or $9 or even $10 price of a single admission ticket and the 100-minute running time of the average film. Unless you're walk-ing to the theater and you're going to avoid the concession counter, the actual price of a single film experience can easily reach the $15 or $20 mark. And as for the time commitment, when was the last time a film with a listed start time of 6 P.M. actually started at 6 P.M.? You know you're going to have to sit through a good ten to fifteen minutes of trivia questions, slide shows, trailers and commercials before the movie starts.

In order to capture the typical twenty-first century moviegoing experience on a weekday evening, let's go to the movies with my friend Paige Wiser, a writer for the *Chicago Sun-Times* and a movie-loving, suburban-dwelling, married mother of one.

First there was the drive: about nine miles from Paige's house in the northwest suburbs to the Loews theaters at the

Streets of Woodfield in Schaumburg. Departure time was 6:03 P.M. for the 7:25 P.M. movie and we got to the free parking garage at 6:29 P.M.

We got tickets at 6:35 P.M. "No line on a Thursday night, which surprises me," said Paige. "So let's do some reporting on the concession stand. It's truly an amazing concession stand. Check it out, you can get piña colada smoothies, bagel dogs, Breyer's ice cream in several flavors, Toll House cookies, gourmet stuffed pretzels, Connie's Pizza and churros."

The prices ranged from the head-shakingly exorbitant ($3.29 for Skittles) to the obscene ($3.99 for a bottle of Dasani water). Some of the high-end items on the menu:

Soft drinks: $3.79, $3.39, $2.89
"Icees": $3.59, $3.99
Bottled Dasani water: $3.99
Popcorn: $4.99 ("value" size)
"Super Value" bucket of popcorn: $5.75
Chicken tenders: $6.25
Funnel cakes: $3.75
Nachos: $4.70
Nachos grande: $7.25
Chili or cheese fries: $5.25
"Gourmet" cheese pizza: $6 ($6.50 for pepperoni or sausage)
Chicken quesadillas: $6.25
Hot dog: $3.99

Chicken tender combo: $8.25
Hot dog and fries combo: $7.25

With the exception of that $4 bottle of water, we're talk-
ing about food often found on the menu in sports bars—
food that'll shorten your life if you eat it on a regular basis.
There's not a single item that could be considered remotely
good for you, and that's pretty consistent with just about
every concession stand at every theater in the country. It's a
junk food orgy out there, and there's little if any consideration given to the fact that a good percentage of moviegoers
are actually interested in healthful foods. Wouldn't it make
economic as well as nutritional sense to stock up the concession stand with some alternative offerings, like low-fat
muffins or fruit or sugar-free smoothies? You'd think a theater would make a killing by offering such popular snacks.

Our admission for two was $17.50. Add to that one
medium Diet Coke (medium being about the size of my
head) for $2.99, one bottle of water for $3.99, one regular
popcorn for $3.99, one gourmet pizza for $6.50 and a $3.29
bag of Skittles, and we're talking about a $38.26 investment.
Throw in a buck and change for the gasoline consumed on
the eighteen-mile round trip and we'll call it an even $40.

"Factoid," announced Paige. "This multiplex has twenty
screens on two levels." At 6:47 she took a bathroom break
and reported back: "I think you should always at least *try* to
go before a movie. I was pretty quick, pausing only to hear
someone babbling to her friend 'Bliss.' Also, there was no

toilet paper in the first stall, so I had to shop around a little bit. You might want to factor in some time for a shy bladder; many women have them. Then you had to find the soap, because not every sink has their little reservoir filled, and then you need some time to figure out how to magically start the water by frantically waving your hands underneath the faucet, arguing with yourself about whether the water is activated by heat or movement."

It's a good thing we'd left her house early.

On the way into the theater, there was a "Cingular Courtesy Zone," a little table with literature on it. Because of course we all want to encourage cell phone use in a movie theater environment as much as possible.

There were also vending machines, and we spent another $2 for Reese's Peanut Butter Cups. So now we were up to $42.

We were in the theater at 7:06 P.M. for the 7:25 movie, and a commercial slide show was already in progress, accompanied by music that sounded like a Gregorian chant. There were also bits of trivia sponsored by the E! channel, and as Paige noted, "These are not very wholesome!" One slide informed us that Halle Berry lost 80 percent of the hearing in one ear from an "abusive boyfriend," and another noted that Jack Nicholson didn't know that his "sister" was actually his mother when he was growing up. A third slide mentioned that Madonna made her film debut at twenty-one in the nude in the low-budget *A Certain Sacrifice*.

The ads were relentless, including slides for Chipotle

Mexican food, the National Dodgeball Championships, Walter E. Smith and Screenvision Direct, which is the company that will sell you ads to run in movie theaters.

There was a name-that-quote panel that said: "Alex, the ceiling is dripping on us." It turned out to be Drew Barrymore from the movie *Duplex*.

"Because 'Alex, the ceiling is dripping on us' is a catchphrase that's really sweeping the nation," said Paige.

The lights lowered at 7:25 P.M., the putative start time for the movie. But it really just marked the transition from the ten-second slide-show ads to actual commercials. The first ad was a plea that we not pirate movies anymore. Next up was the "Coca-Cola Refreshing Filmmaker" award-winner, a little movie about a *Sopranos*-type crime family running a movie theater. Roughing up customers, pressuring people to buy the bigger size Coke, that sort of thing. It was mildly amusing.

Next was a Cingular ad, which had a funny bit about a phone ringing in a theater, and then the guy getting ejected from his seat and getting splattered on the screen. It said: "Cell phone ejector seats: Soon coming to a theater near you. For your own safety, please silence your cell phones."

Then there was an ad for the Fandango web site, where you can buy tickets online. Instead of using people, they use real people's voices, and show brown-paper-bag puppets mouthing the words onscreen.

Next was an ad for the "*Cat in the Hat* Loews Gift Card."

Then an ad for the Army National Guard.

Then a spot for www.earnfreemovies.com.

At 7:31, the lights were further dimmed, for previews. First up: *Timeline* ("Think of it as the ultimate field trip"). Then Jennifer Connelly and Ben Kingsley in *House of Sand and Fog*. Then *The Last Samurai*, and *Cheaper by the Dozen* (Paige: "Steve Martin must want to buy another beach house"), followed by *Love Actually* and *Master and Commander*.

At 7:44, we got the "Loews Enjoy the Show!" promotion, and at 7:45 P.M. the lights were finally dimmed to the level of soothing near-darkness, and the movie began.

At 9:47 P.M., *Runaway Jury* ended, with Paige lauding the film and noting that Dustin Hoffman's southern-lawyer voice was a repeat of his *Tootsie* voice. By 10:12 P.M., the trip home had been completed.

So we're talking about an investment of four hours and forty-two bucks. As it happens, I liked *Runaway Jury*—more for the performances by Dustin Hoffman, Gene Hackman and John Cusack than for the typically outrageous plot from the Grisham factory—but it's the kind of film you can wait to rent. Spend $3 at the video store, microwave your own popcorn and drink water that doesn't cost *four dollars a bottle*, and the investment would be about equal to the level of entertainment.

This is why I can't be too concerned with the egos and

feelings of the director and the producer and the writer and the actors when I'm writing up a review. If two people have to invest about four hours and $42 for the typical moviegoing experience, the least they deserve is an unblinking opinion from their neighborhood critic.

Politics and the Movies

From *The Passion of the Christ* to *Fahrenheit 9/11,* movie-related controversies were front-page news in 2004 more often than in any year in my lifetime.

For months prior to its release, Mel Gibson's deeply personal retelling of the last twelve hours of Jesus' life attracted worldwide attention. Without having seen the finished product, some Jewish leaders and op-ed writers condemned the film as anti-Semitic and predicted it would promote violence against Jews. Gibson, in a masterstroke of playing both sides against the middle, set up screenings of rough cuts of the film all over the world—and then professed to being shocked that some religious leaders had problems with it. Unable to get financing from any of the major studios, Gibson reportedly committed some $25 million of his own money to the project—a move that turned out to be one of the wisest investments in the history of motion pictures.

After the film was released, some critics found strains of

anti-Semitism in Gibson's portrayal of the Jewish high priests who plotted and angled for the crucifixion of Jesus—but there wasn't a single report of someone seeing the film and then committing an anti-Semitic act. The debate quickly shifted to whether *The Passion of the Christ* was gratuitously violent, with its excruciatingly lengthy scenes of the scourging and crucifixion of Jesus.

It was fascinating that so many people were stunned and offended by the admittedly rough content. As related in the gospels, the "passion" of Christ is a reference to the pain he endured for all humankind. This is what the film is about: Christ's suffering. Yet there was much hand-wringing over the content of *The Passion* while we continued to shrug our shoulders at cartoonishly violent films where human beings are beaten, kicked, blown up, shot, stabbed, strangled, run over, disemboweled and/or decapitated, all in the name of escapist entertainment. Entertainment that's often rated PG-13, I might add.

A number of films released in 2004, including *Van Helsing, The Chronicles of Riddick, Hellboy, Walking Tall* and *King Arthur* are filled with intense, brutal action and multiple acts of murder and violence—yet all attained the commercially friendly PG-13 rating.

Perhaps the most shocking thing about *The Passion of the Christ* was its box office performance. As of this writing, it's the No. 1 R-rated film and the No. 8 film overall on the domestic box office charts, with a gross of $370 million. (*The Passion* has made another $230 million internationally.) Adjusted for inflation, *The Passion of the Christ* is No. 50 overall, but that still places it well ahead of such classic blockbusters as *West Side Story, My Fair Lady* and *Rocky.* Amazing.

And to think Gibson had such trouble finding financial backers for his seemingly risky project. Still, despite the jaw-dropping box office performance of his film, there's no truth to the rumor Mel is working on a sequel titled, *Jesus: Reloaded.*

And then came *Fahrenheit 9/11,* Michael Moore's deeply personal, wildly unfair and hugely entertaining criticism of the Bush administration. This is when you know a documentary has entered uncharted territory: In July of 2004, I was lounging poolside at the Moorea Beach Club in Mandalay Bay, the kind of place where there's a cover charge just to walk in, and "European style" (that means topless) sunbathing is permitted. And there, on a most glorious and sultry summer day, a beautiful young woman wearing virtually nothing was standing waist-deep in the soothing cool water, SCREAMING at a man she'd just met.

"I can't believe you're saying it's a great film," she exclaimed. "Michael Moore is BIASED! The whole thing is just his opinion, and he hates Bush. He just makes things up! I'm not giving ten dollars of my money to that fat f—."

Which is pretty much what Fox News was saying about *Fahrenheit 9/11.*

Ever the master showman, Moore embraced and enhanced every controversy that came his way, starting with his claim that he was being "censored" by Disney because the studio wouldn't release the film. Of all people, Michael Moore should know that corporations don't censor—governments do. In any case, Moore, Harvey Weinstein and Lion's Gate partnered to distributed the movie, which became a huge hit.

Of course Moore is biased. Has he ever pretended to be neutral? Of course he's presenting his opinions. Of course *Fahrenheit 9/11* isn't a documentary in the tradition of the Maysles brothers. Like *Roger and Me* and *Bowling for Columbine,* it's an immensely effective piece of nonfiction performance art, with Moore finessing the facts to fit his point of view. In other words, Moore is to the documentary what Rush Limbaugh is to radio and Bill O'Reilly is to the one-hour news-talk show—a tremendously talented performer who presents every story through the filter of his own personal and political views.

After I gave *Fahrenheit 9/11* a glowing review, I heard from hundreds of conservatives who told me I was delusional if I believed the film was a documentary. I don't know how to break this to you, folks—but if and when the movie gets nominated for an Academy Award, it's not going to be in the Animated category.

On the day *Fahrenheit 9/11* opened across the country, I found myself in the middle of a controversy.

From Page Six the *New York Post*: "Censorship is alive

and well and rearing its ugly head through the [MPAA]. Richard Roeper's comment on *Fahrenheit 9/11*—'Everyone should see this film'—has been banned from the movie's ads by the MPAA because it carries an R rating. The MPAA wouldn't back down, even after Lion's Gate Films, Miramax and Roeper appealed. 'They don't trust their own ratings system,' an outraged Roeper told PAGE SIX's Lisa Marsh. 'If their system worked, everyone under seventeen would be stopped anyway . . . '"

Weinstein issued a statement that said, in part: "Everyone knows that Richard Roeper did not call for anyone to violate the R rating, and this ruling is a huge disservice to the public."

Newspapers from Los Angeles to India wrote about the dustup. In the *Sunday Times* of London, Michael Wright wrote, "Congratulations to the Motion Picture Association of America for nit-picking in the face of adversity. When the U.S. film critic Richard Roeper reviewed *Fahrenheit 9/11* and declared that 'Everyone should see this movie,' the film's distributors delightedly chose to print his encomium on their posters. But that didn't go down with the MPAA, which banned the quote . . . because, as it pointed out, the 'R' rating it slapped on the film means that not everyone should see it. So there."

To set the record straight: I was hardly "outraged" when I talked to Page Six, though I did say I thought it was ridiculous for the MPAA to squash the quote. I said what I said and I meant what I said.

But this wasn't about censorship. Studios that submit their films for ratings must abide by the MPAA's ridiculously rigid advertising guidelines, which assume a certain amount of stupidity on the part of the consumer. Obviously I wasn't saying, "Nine-year-olds should sneak into this film, and toddlers should see it too!"

The movie was rated R. It's now out on DVD. Parents can decide for themselves if their children should see it—although by the time most kids are twelve, they've already seen much more violent material than anything contained in *Fahrenheit 9/11*.

Liberal-hating political pundit Ann Coulter's shtick is to blame every problem in the history of the world on liberals, whom she hates with a passion that couldn't be explained with a thousand hours of intense therapy. In her best-selling books and her endless TV appearances, Coulter attacks liberals with such cartoonishly simplistic generalizations that one can only chuckle at her madness. Just a few examples:

"Even Islamic terrorists don't hate America like liberals do."

"The [Ku Klux] Klan sees the world in terms of race and ethnicity. So do liberals!"

"Everyone knows it's an insult to be called a liberal, widely understood to connote a dastardly individual."

You get the idea.

Coulter's hatred has a way of blinding her to the facts and leaving her in a fantasy world in which history is ignored, even when she's talking about movies. On November 4, 2003, Coulter was on MSNBC's *Hardball with Chris Matthews* to discuss *The Reagans*, the controversial miniseries that CBS dumped off to the premium cable channel Showtime after conservatives howled long and hard about the supposedly offensive portrayal of their beloved Ron and Nancy. (In truth, the final product was a standard biopic that was far less harsh than numerous television movies we've seen about the Kennedy family.) The talk turned to another famous political family.

MATTHEWS: *"Let me ask you, Ann Coulter. Do you think the Clintons would make a good—what do you call it—a good property for a mini-series? And could it be done fairly?"*

COULTER: *"It would have been done, if it had been done honestly, I think extremely well. And I agree with you that they're capable of doing an honest movie that extrapolates slightly but basically gets the characters right. And I'll give you an example of one where they did it with hatred in their hearts, but unfortunately, they did it accurate to history, and that was* Patton. *That was intended to make Patton look terrible, but it was accurate to history and it made Patton look great and people loved him. And that's why they don't do it accurately anymore."*

MATTHEWS: *"You are dead wrong. Everybody loved* Patton *from the first day it came out."*

COULTER: *"But that isn't the way it was intended."*

MATTHEWS: *"I was in the Peace Corps in Africa and everybody over there loved it when we got to see it. From the first day we loved it."*

DAVID CORN [ANOTHER GUEST ON THE PROGRAM]: *"How could you not love that movie from the opening scene?"*

MATTHEWS: *"He's God-like. Ann, where do you get this malarkey from? Everybody loved* Patton. *How old were you, when* Patton *came out? How old were you, two?"*

COULTER: *"I think you're misunderstanding."*

MATTHEWS: *"No, I think you're wrong, Ann. I think everybody loved* Patton.*"*

COULTER: *"Can I respond?"*

MATTHEWS: *"Who didn't like it?"*

COULTER: *"That is precisely my point, because it was made accurately. But when it was made, the people making it were intending to make Patton look bad."*

Let's take a break from Annie's fantasy scenario and examine the facts. Coulter says people made *Patton* "with hatred in their hearts." Maybe she's talking about the film's producer, Frank McCarthy, whose liberal resume begins with his graduation from the Virginia Military Institute in 1933. McCarthy was a brigadier general who served as an aide to General George C. Marshall during World War II and spent two decades of his life trying to get a film made about General George S. Patton.

Or perhaps Coulter was referring to General Omar Bradley, whose book *A Soldier's Story* was one of the two main sources for the screenplay, which was cowritten by Francis Ford Coppola. (The other source was Ladislas Fargo's *Patton: Ordeal and Triumph*.) Bradley served as the film's official technical military adviser, no doubt with hatred in his heart.

I suppose Coulter could be talking about 20th Century–Fox, or director Franklin J. Schaffner, or the guy who dispensed donuts and coffee on the set—but the reality is that *Patton* was an epic and respectful biography of the mercurial general, and there's no evidence in the source materials, the screenplay or the film itself that the idea was to "make Patton look terrible," as Coulter asserted on MSNBC. For God's sake, the film opens with the famous six-minute scene of Patton in full military dress, his uniform festooned with ribbons and medals as he struts in front of a screen-filling American flag and waxes eloquent about the glory of war. *Patton* was one of the major film events of 1970, a critical success and commercial smash with an adjusted-for-inflation gross of $254 million, and a slew of Oscars including Best Picture. (Robert Altman's antiwar *M*A*S*H*, also a huge hit, was one of the Best Picture nominees that year, losing out to the more traditional *Patton*.) The film was said to be a favorite of Richard Nixon's, who watched it repeatedly for patriotic inspiration in the White House.

One can only wonder: Has Ann Coulter ever *seen* this movie? Has she so much as glanced at a clip from it?

Instead of actually listening to Matthews' legitimate challenges and realizing she should just shut her trap—which would be a career first—Coulter continued bending the truth to the breaking point:

> COULTER: *"The people making [the movie] were intending to make Patton look bad . . . That is why George C. Scott turned down his Academy Award for playing Patton."*
>
> MATTHEWS: *"Who told you that? Who told you that?"*
>
> COULTER: *"It's well known."*
>
> MATTHEWS: *"It's well known?"*
>
> COULTER: *"Why do you think he didn't accept the award?"*
>
> CORN: *"Why did he take the role? Why did he take the role, Ann, if he didn't want to do it?"*
>
> COULTER: *"Why do you think he turned down the award, Chris? You never looked that up? It never occurred to you? 'I wonder why George C. Scott didn't accept his award.'"*
>
> MATTHEWS: *"Because he said he wasn't going to a meat parade, because he didn't believe in award ceremonies because they're all about women wearing no clothes and showing off their bodies . . ."*
>
> COULTER: *"By portraying Patton as negatively as possible—but by doing it accurately the American people loved it."*
>
> MATTHEWS: *"Facts mean nothing to you, Ann."*

CORN: *"In this movie he shoots down an airplane with a gun."*

MATTHEWS: *"I'm glad you are not making movies, Ann Coulter. Thank you, David Corn, Andrew Grossman. Jesus."*

Kudos to *Hardball* host Matthews for living up to his show's name and not allowing Coulter to prattle on with her insanely fictional scenario. If Coulter herself had bothered to look it up, she would have learned that George C. Scott was distancing himself from acting awards as early as 1961, when he refused to accept his nomination for Best Supporting Actor for *The Hustler* (he didn't win) and said the Oscars were "a weird beauty or personality contest." A decade later, Scott refused to accept even the nomination for *Patton* and said he would refuse the trophy if he won. "The ceremonies are a two-hour meat parade, a public display with contrived suspense for economic reasons," said Scott. On the night of the Oscars, Scott was at home in New York, watching a hockey game on TV. When Goldie Hawn opened the envelope and screamed, "Oh my God, the winner is George C. Scott!" it was *Patton*'s producer, retired Brigadier General Frank McCarthy, who accepted the award and thanked the Academy. But in accordance with Scott's wishes, McCarthy returned the award the following day.

Coulter's version of events is pure fiction. Either she was ignorant or she was deliberately lying. Either way, it didn't stop her from spouting off like a fool on *Hardball*—and no doubt some viewers believed she was being truthful. After all, even a liberal-hating harridan wouldn't just make up things, right?

Not that hard-right conservatives have a monopoly on idiotic commentary about the movies; liberals can be myopic and shrill too. Consider the great *Barbershop* debate, one of the most ridiculous controversies in recent history. When I saw the film in September 2002, a few weeks before its theatrical release, I had two reactions:

A. The movie was hilarious and heartfelt, with a lively script and a wonderful ensemble cast, and it was destined to become a hit.

B. There was going to be trouble.

The day before the film opened, my *Chicago Sun-Times* column was devoted to *Barbershop*, and in particular Cedric the Entertainer's movie-stealing performance as Eddie, the old-school barber who's been working from the same chair for more than thirty years and spends precious little time actually cutting hair because he's too busy marveling at the sound of his own voice. Eddie is a comic character who munches on fried chicken and mispronounces "reparations" as "respirations"—but his showcase moment comes when he lectures the barbershop with some painfully blunt opinions about race relations.

"Black people need to stop lying!" says Eddie. "There's

three things that black people need to tell the truth about. One, Rodney King got his ass beat for driving drunk . . . in a Hyundai. Two, O.J. did it. And three, Rosa Parks didn't do nothing but sit her black ass down [on that bus]."

And when Jesse Jackson's name is brought into the discussion, Eddie retorts: "Fuck Jesse Jackson!"

In context, you realize that Eddie believes maybe half of what he's saying. More important, he's obviously trying to get a rise out of the younger barbers—to get them to think about recent history and to expand the conversation beyond money and women and women and money.

"Is this a barbershop?" says Eddie. "Is this a barbershop? If we can't talk straight in a barbershop, then where can we talk straight? We can't talk straight nowhere else. You know this ain't nothing but healthy conversation."

In my column I wrote:

> And that's the small glory of this film—the honesty that bounces off those walls. *Barbershop* isn't a "black movie," it's a movie about interesting, three-dimensional, smart and hilariously opinionated black people . . . [it] isn't just for blacks any more than *My Big Fat Greek Wedding* is just for Greeks. . . .
>
> It'll be interesting to see how *Barbershop* plays—not just with full-time film critics of all races, but with black commentators and community leaders, and with the moviegoing public. Will they find it to be an honest celebration of the longtime significance of the neighborhood

barbershop—or a stereotype-laden chuckle fest with a self-loathing character who criticizes his own people?

In less than a week, we had our answer. *Barbershop* opened to great reviews (according to the Rotten Tomatoes web site, out of more than 100 reviews, 84 percent were positive) and $20 million in its opening weekend—but Jesse Jackson and other black leaders were complaining about Cedric the Entertainer's Eddie character.

" 'Barbershop' Dialogue Too Cutting, Some Say," was the headline in *USA Today*, which quoted Jackson as saying, "The filmmakers crossed the line between what's sacred and serious and what's funny . . . There are some heroes who are sacred to a people, and these comments poisoned an otherwise funny movie. Why put cyanide in the Kool-Aid?"

Jackson, who said he had received angry calls from Al Sharpton, Martin Luther King III and others, later called for the supposedly offensive scene to be deleted from the DVD version of *Barbershop*. Never mind that he hadn't actually seen the movie, as he admitted during an interview on the *John Williams Show* on WGN-AM radio in Chicago; why should he let a little thing like not knowing what he's talking about stop him from protesting the movie and calling for the filmmakers to censor themselves for the video release?

As *Barbershop* marched to an impressive $75 million box-office total, there were literally hundreds of stories about Cedric's monologue. One could track the evolution of the controversy, starting with my September 12, 2002, pre–

opening day column, titled, "'Ain't nobody exempt in the barbershop,'" through the newspaper headlines and TV subject categories in the following weeks. It's like one of those old movie montages where they move the plot along by spinning several headlines in a row:

> Copley News Service, September 25: "Nothing is Sacred in a Barbershop"
>
> CNN *Crossfire*, September 25: "Should Blacks Boycott *Barbershop*?"
>
> *CBS Evening News with Dan Rather*, September 25: "Controversy over the movie *Barbershop* among civil rights leaders."
>
> *Washington Post*, September 26: "MGM Stands by Beleaguered *Barbershop*; Sharpton, Others Claim Hit Film Disparages Civil Rights Icons"
>
> *Milwaukee Journal Sentinel*, September 26: "Barbers' Advice to Jesse: Lighten up"
>
> Associated Press, September 26: "MGM Announces *Barbershop* Sequel; Says It Won't Edit Original"
>
> *Slate* Magazine, September 27: "Is *Barbershop* Right About Rosa Parks?"
>
> New York *Daily News*, September 29: "Jackson and Sharpton Are Looking Irrelevant: Why Do They Protest a Harmless Movie?"
>
> *Ft. Lauderdale Sun-Sentinel*, October 2: "*Barbershop* Uproar Ignores Real World"

I can't think of another mainstream, upbeat comedy that's ever generated such a prolonged and heated debate—

but I don't think it's unreasonable to ask that before one offers an opinion about a movie, one should actually SEE THE DAMN THING, whether you're a social activist or a media commentator. Believe it or not, the lead news columnist for the *Chicago Tribune* criticized Jackson for complaining about *Barbershop* without having seen it—and then admitted that he hadn't seen it either. He even related a conversation with the *Tribune*'s film critic, who questioned how he could write about the film without having seen it. The response: "Well . . . I'm not writing about the film, exactly. I'm writing about Jackson going ballistic about the film." Great. So we have a columnist who hasn't seen a movie, writing about a civil rights leader who hasn't seen the movie either. Anyone else want blinders?

There's nothing more ridiculous than activists who protest a movie without having actually seen the film. Here's a partial list of films that have drawn picket lines and protests, often prior to their release dates, and the offenses, real or imagined:

> *Monty Python's The Meaning of Life* (1983)—
>   sacrilegious
> *Colors* (1988)—promotes gang violence
> *The Last Temptation of Christ* (1988)—anti-Jesus

Silence of the Lambs (1991)—homophobic

JFK (1991)—blatant distortion of history

The Pope Must Die (1991; retitled *The Pope Must Diet*)—anti-Catholic

Basic Instinct (1992)—homophobic

Natural Born Killers (1994)—glorified serial killers

Priest (1994)—anti-Catholic

Dogma (1999)—anti-Christian

The Siege (1998)—anti-Islamic

The Believer (2002)—anti-Semitic

Barbershop (2002)—disparages civil rights icons

The Crime of Father Amaro (2002)—anti-Catholic

The Passion of the Christ (2004)—anti-Semitic; gratuitously violent

THE WAY THINGS REALLY ARE

In his 1992 mega-selling book *The Way Things Ought to Be*, Rush Limbaugh turned movie critic, writing, "Hollywood is in trouble . . . Hollywood has forgotten who its audience is. It now makes a lot of movies that disparage American institutions and traditions or which promote wacko leftism. Hollywood has become part of the dominant media culture. They love to make fun of what people like you and I hold dear. They make fun of people who believe in God. They ridicule the traditional family, heterosexuality and monogamy. They disparage American heroes."

I like the idea that Limbaugh in 1992 decided "Hollywood has become part of the dominant media culture." As opposed to the 1920s or the 1940s, when Hollywood was only hoping to become a small part of the media culture?

As for Limbaugh's other assertions: Let's take a look at the No. 1 movies in each of the years since Limbaugh's comments. The box-office champs include the family-friendly *Aladdin* (1992), *Toy Story* (1995), *Harry Potter* (2001) and *Finding Nemo* (2003); *Forrest Gump* (1994), a film that was publicly embraced by a number of high-profile conservatives, including Limbaugh; the jingoistic *Independence Day* (1996); four old-fashioned and hardly subversive fantasy adventures in *Jurassic Park* (1993), *The Phantom Menace* (1999), *The Grinch* (2000) and *Spider-Man* (2002); one historical romance, *Titanic* (1997); and *Saving Private Ryan* (1998), Steven Spielberg's powerful and deeply respectful tribute to the American soldiers who fought in World War II.

Limbaugh's generalizations are also defeated by the list of Best Picture winners from 1992 through 2003: *Unforgiven*, *Schindler's List*, *Forrest Gump*, *Braveheart*, *The English Patient*, *Titanic*, *Shakespeare in Love*, *American Beauty*, *Gladiator*, *A Beautiful Mind*, *Chicago*, and *The Lord of the Rings: Return of the King*. With the exception of the dark *American Beauty*, most of the Best Picture winners have either been Limbaugh-friendly macho action pics such as *Unforgiven*, *Braveheart* and *Gladiator*, or stories about brave heroes who overcome great adversity, e.g., *Schindler's List*, *Forrest Gump* and *A Beautiful Mind*.

No doubt Limbaugh will soon revisit his old assessment and embrace Hollywood for having made so many recent Oscar winners that are patriotic, inspirational and/or family friendly.

CELEBRITIES AND POLITICS

Many celebrities are educated, well informed, dedicated citizens who sound off on political issues only after carefully sifting through the facts and forming a sound, reasonable opinion. Others are egotistical blowhards who can't resist the sound of their own voices and are infused with such narcissism that they believe being rich, pretty and famous means the world is breathlessly awaiting their views on the weightiest matters imaginable. Some of the more astounding celebrity quotes in recent history:

"And I have come back from Africa to stained dresses and cigars . . . and impeachment. In other countries they are laughing at us twenty-four hours a day and I'm thinking to myself, if we were in other countries, we would all right now, all of us together, all of us together would go down to Washington and we would stone Henry Hyde to death! We would stone him to death! Wait! Shut up! Shut up! No shut up. I'm not finished. We should stone Henry Hyde to death and we would go to their homes and we'd kill their wives and children. We would kill their families. What is happening in this country! What is happening!"—Alec Baldwin on *Late Night with Conan O'Brien*, in a grotesquely unfunny attempt to comment on the Clinton impeachment proceedings.

"Charlton Heston announced again today that he is suffering from Alzheimer's."—the normally cool and smooth George Clooney, making a tasteless joke about a political rival.

"I hate Bush. I despise him and his entire administration . . . what Bush intends to do with Iraq is unconstitutional, immoral and illegal."—Jessica Lange, playing right into the hands of conservatives who believe the Hollywood elite actually hates the president. Wouldn't it be more intelligent and effective to say something like, "I hate terrorism and I hate what was done to my country on September 11, but I also believe that what Bush intends to do with Iraq is unconstitutional, immoral and illegal"?

"I didn't know that 6 million Jews were killed. That's a lot of people."—Melanie Griffith, explaining to reporters that she had just learned an amazing true fact about the Holocaust.

"I was on my way to Australia when [the attacks] happened, and they told me what happened, but I didn't really understand until I got up and I looked at the TV and I was like, 'Oh my God, is this like freaking *Independence Day*?' It was just like a movie or something."—Britney Spears at a press conference, explaining her reaction to the attacks of September 11, 2001.

The Unreleased Film Festival

One of the more effective performances by any actress in 2003 was turned in by Busy Phillips, a young actress best known for her TV work on *Dawson's Creek* and *Freaks and Geeks*. Phillips played a cynical, emotionally scarred Goth outcast in *Home Room*, first-time writer/director Paul F. Ryan's intense, character-driven set piece that focuses on the aftermath of a Columbine-like shooting in a suburban high school that leaves nine dead, including the lone teenage gunman. Parents of the victims and community leaders pressure the lead investigative detective, played by Victor Garber, to find out if anyone in the school knew about the gunman's plans—and his best and only lead is Phillips' sullen, Marlboro-smoking, heavily pierced, perpetually scowling Alicia, who spoke on the phone for an hour with the shooter on the night before his rampage. Did she have advance warning? And if so, why didn't she tell anyone?

Already twenty years old, having missed a year and a half

of school for reasons unfolded later in the film, Alicia is seriously lost. She's so numb to the shootings that she shows up at school the next morning with her backpack and her piercings and her shocking white hair and her thick makeup, only to be met at the entrance by the incredulous principal, who explains the obvious—that the school has literally been shot up, and it will be a long time before the doors reopen. Physical repairs must be made; wounds of all kinds must be given time to heal. Realizing that if left on her own Alicia will disappear, the principal creates an assignment that will help Alicia improve her spotty academic record and keep her off the streets: She will spend time every day with Deanna (Erika Christensen from *Traffic* and *Swimfan*), a chatty, straight-A student who remains relentlessly upbeat in a manic-cheerleader kind of way, even as she lies in a hospital bed with her head half-shaved, recovering from a gunshot wound as well as a simmering case of post-traumatic stress syndrome.

The rebellious Alicia has only resentment and disdain for the book-smart, super-achieving Deanna, who in turn is fascinated by Alicia's outlaw persona. It's the relationship between these two girls that forms the heart of *Home Room*. Prior to the shootings, they wouldn't have said hello to each other in the hallways—but Alicia was standing next to the gunman when he was killed, and Deanna survived being shot at close range, and from this one horrible, irretractable, life-shattering incident, they form a bond that yields surprising revelations from both sides. For every poignant moment that threatens to sink *Home Room* in melodrama (e.g., when

Deanna cries, "I'm dying inside!"), there's a much-needed dose of effectively-dark humor, as when the sheltered Deanna asks Alicia about the pain involved in losing one's virginity and Alicia deadpans, "It's not as bad as getting shot in the head." Christensen is strong and sympathetic as the success-oriented yet lonely Deanna, but it's Phillips who has the showcase role as the self-styled weirdo who deflects intimacy with her confrontationally outrageous appearance and her biting sarcasm. As the smart but wounded Alicia, Phillips spouts one-liners with the acid-tongued delivery of a stand-up comedienne, but occasionally her eyes betray her and we see that this is a girl who has been through hell; she's still hurting from incidents not yet revealed. It's a beautiful and raw piece of acting.

Home Room also benefits from strong performances by Garber as the detective who refuses to ruin another life in the interest of appeasing a community in mourning; Holland Taylor as a hospital psychiatrist; and Agnes Bruckner from *Blue Car* as another surviving classmate. As a director, Ryan indulges his own screenplay to a fault, and *Home Room* could have been even more effective if he had trimmed about twenty minutes from the 126-minute running time. Still, this film is a sincere, unblinking exploration of the all-too-familiar subject of high school massacres that begins when the shootings end, and Phillips gives a breakout performance.

And you're thinking, "What is this guy talking about? What is this movie and who is this actress and when did it come out and how come I never heard about it?"

Home Room is a classic example of a Lost Movie—a film that is conceived as a commercial, theatrical release, but gets sidetracked somewhere along the way and is either dumped into a few theaters with the promotional volume on "mute," or goes straight to video or premium cable. You'll be wandering the outer aisles of the local video store, or you'll be clicking around the dial late one night, and you'll come across a movie featuring a hot young commodity such as Jared Leto, Jake Gyllenhaal, Mandy Moore, Elijah Wood, Leonardo DiCaprio or Selma Blair, or a popular star such as Russell Crowe, Sandra Bullock, Salma Hayek, Kevin Spacey or Billy Bob Thornton, or an established veteran such as Anthony Hopkins, Kathy Bates, Sylvester Stallone or Michael Caine—and you'll never have heard of this movie. Even after you read the plot summary on the back of the DVD case or you check the *TV Guide* or activate the onscreen information button, the title and the plot ring no bells.

You've stumbled upon a Lost Movie.

Films are scattered to the winds of obscurity for all sorts of reasons. A studio collapses, and its library of unreleased films gets stuck in limbo. A low-budget movie with recognizable actors makes a splash at one or two film festivals, but never finds a distributor. A director and a studio chief get into a tug of war over "creative differences" that's never resolved, even after rewrites and reshoots, and the finished product lingers in a vault. Or maybe there's a real-life tragedy with eerie parallels to a film, and it would be bad timing and bad taste to release the movie.

But what happens most often is this: The studio executives see the finished product and decide the film has shaky commercial prospects. They decide to cut their losses rather than throw good money after bad. Why invest millions more in distribution and marketing if unanimous corporate opinion indicates the film will tank? If no other studio indicates interest in picking up the project, the movie might be released in some overseas markets but never in the United States, or it'll be dumped into a few theaters in the States for an extremely limited run with no advertising support. Sometimes the film is never racked on a single commercial projector and is exiled straight to video or to one of the premium cable channels.

In 1999, Ben Affleck and Matt Damon executive produced *The Third Wheel*, a romantic comedy starring Luke Wilson and Denise Richards, with supporting appearances by Affleck and Damon. According to a *Daily Variety* article from 1999, Wilson and Richards played "doomed lovers . . . who are thwarted in their efforts to enjoy an evening together by a third wheel (Jay Lacopo)." Miramax picked up the U.S. and some foreign distribution rights, with chairman Harvey Weinstein telling *Variety*, "I am proud to be continuing our relationship with Matt and Ben on another great project."

Nearly four years later, Weinstein was singing a different

tune about the film, which still hadn't been released. In a March 7, 2003, interview, a reporter for *Entertainment Weekly* asked Weinstein, "What happened to *Third Wheel*?"

"It's going to be sold to television, where it belongs," came the curt reply.

In April 2004 *The Third Wheel* was finally released—on video.

The Lost Movie is not a new phenomenon. The history of cinema is filled with stories of productions that started and stopped and floundered for years before crashing under the weight of their own ambitions, and ill-conceived vanity projects that crumbled in spectacular fashion—and movies that just plain sucked and were buried in the interest of good taste. Some Lost Movies are eventually "found." Others remain the stuff of legend. Here are a few of the most infamous Lost Movies of all time.

THE OTHER SIDE OF THE WIND

(Filmed from 1970 to 1975; never released)—In 1970, thirteen years after Orson Welles had directed his last mainstream film, he began shooting a film-within-a-film about a once-great director (played by John Huston) who launches one last comeback. (Yet Welles claimed it wasn't the least bit autobiographical.) Welles shot the wildly experimental film in dribs and drabs over a five-year period, assembling cast and crew whenever he had raised enough funds from TV guest appearances and commercials to continue shooting. A finished product was never released, but there have been private screenings of a version that was edited after Welles' death, and excerpts were featured in a 2003 documentary about Welles that aired on Showtime.

THE OUTLAW
(Filmed in 1941, released in 1943)—It took two years for this racy film starring Jane Russell and Jane Russell's cleavage to pass muster with the Hollywood Production Code. Were it released today, *The Outlaw* would probably get a PG rating.

OTHELLO
(Filmed from 1948 to 1951; released in 1952)—Another experimental and greatly troubled project from Orson Welles that was filmed over several years. The "completed" version still looked unfinished.

THE DAY THE CLOWN CRIED
(Filmed in 1972; never released)—Jerry Lewis directed himself in this oft-discussed but rarely seen film about Helmut Doork, a German circus clown who is arrested for making fun of Hitler. Doork is sent to a concentration camp and is forced to keep the children entertained as he leads them to the ovens. Principal photography was done in Stockholm, but the producer ran out of money, and Lewis used his own

funds to complete filming. The movie has been tied up in litigation for three decades, with the original print reportedly stored in a vault in Sweden. To this day, only a lucky few have ever seen even a rough cut of *The Day the Clown Cried*— but at least one version of the original screenplay has circulated on the Internet. Based on that screenplay and accounts from those who claim to have seen the film (including actor/writer Harry Shearer), *The Day the Clown Cried* is heartstopping in its awfulness.

BLUE SKY

(Filmed in 1991; released in 1994)—One of about ten completed films that were left in limbo when Orion filed for bankruptcy in 1991. The film was finally released three years later—and in a bizarre twist, Jessica Lange won Best Actress for her performance as the disturbed wife of a career military man. By that time, the film's director, Tony Richardson, had passed away.

THE FANTASTIKS

(Filmed in 1994; released in 2000)—Michael Ritchie's movie adaptation of one of the most popular stage musicals in history gathered dust for half a dozen years before Francis Ford Coppola trimmed it by twenty-four minutes. After a limited release in a handful of cities, *The Fantastiks* quickly went to video.

TOWN & COUNTRY

(Filmed in 1998; released in 2001)—After countless script revisions and reshoots, this big-budget romantic comedy starring Warren Beatty, Diane Keaton and Goldie Hawn was finally dumped into theaters—and it was as bad as advertised.

On April 10, 2003, Paul Ryan and actress Erika Christensen screened *Home Room* for a special audience at the AMC movie complex in Highlands Ranch, Colorado.

"Director Paul Ryan received two thumbs up Thursday for his film *Home Room* from the critics he cared about most," reported the *Denver Post*. "Some 300 graduating seniors, parents and teachers from Columbine High School applauded loudly as the credits rolled on the first-time director's look at the aftermath of a killing spree patterned on Columbine."

According to the article, the screening was arranged after Columbine English teacher Carol Samson had seen *Home Room* in October 2002 at the Denver Film Festival and had met with Ryan and asked him to show it to the Class of '03.

After the special screening for students, parents and teachers, the *Post* reported that Samson told Ryan, "I tell the kids, 'Beware of the poets who tell our stories,' and plainly our stories are in very good hands with you."

Home Room had played at other festivals in 2002, winning the Audience Award at the Santa Cruz Film Festival and taking home the Grand Jury Prize at the Chamizal Film Festival. Granted, we're not talking about the Palme d'Or at Cannes—but any recognition or award is a boost to a $500,000 film from a first-time director.

In September 2003, *Home Room* was set for a limited theatrical release. The New York Daily News' crabby and hopelessly out of touch Jack Mathews panned the film, while the *Hollywood Reporter*'s Kirk Honeycutt gave it a mixed review but lauded Phillips, noting that she's "up to the challenge" of "making Alicia's past traumas . . . credible and deeply moving." Denver's *Westword* newspaper weighed in with a rave, as did a few online sites and the "Hot Ticket" review program.

As for *Ebert & Roeper*: To my great regret, we didn't review the film. As much as we try to consider every movie that's receiving any kind of theatrical release (and even some direct-to-cable films), *Home Room* didn't make the cut. I'm not sure it was ever brought up for discussion. Some filmmakers and publicists are very aggressive about making us aware of smaller films in limited release, even offering to send us the film on a screener tape in advance. In other cases, it's Roger or I or someone on the staff who becomes aware of a film and pursues it as a possibility for the show. (Usually the representatives of a movie are thrilled to send a screener copy or to set up a showing—but sometimes they don't want us to see the movie because the real hope is that it goes away quietly.) I can't say with 100 percent certainty that nobody approached us about *Home Room*, but I don't recall any press releases or pitches, and it doesn't appear on our screening calendar for August or September of 2003. Given that I visited and wrote about Columbine after the shootings, that I'm always interested in small, dialogue-driven films that explore the unique problems faced by American youth and that I'm a fan of Erika Christensen's work, I can say that that had I been aware of *Home Room*, I would have volunteered to screen it for the show—and it would have ended up on the show with at least one recommendation. Unfortunately, I didn't become aware of *Home Room* until I started doing research for this book, and its theatrical run was over.

In any case, *Home Room* was saddled with one of the worst opening dates in any given year: Labor Day weekend, the official dead zone between the "fun" summer movie season and the "serious" fall movie season. On September 5, 2003, the only new mainstream releases arriving in theaters were *Dickie Roberts: Former Child Star*, a cheap comedy starring David Spade; and *The Order*, a supernatural religious thriller starring Heath Ledger that had been plagued by rumors of a disastrous shoot. (Based on the final product, those rumors were solid.) Obviously, the studios do not waste favored product on Labor Day weekend.

Also dropped into the mix that weekend was *Home Room*, which opened on exactly four screens: Cinema Village and AMC Theaters Empire 25 in New York City; Landmark's

Westside Pavilion Cinemas in West Los Angeles; and the Starz Film Center at the Tivoli in Denver.

Dickie Roberts opened at No. 1 with $6.7 million—a figure that wouldn't crack the top three on many other weekends. *The Order* had an even softer opening weekend of $4.4 million, barely outperforming films that had been in circulation for half the summer and behind such holdovers as *Pirates of the Caribbean*, then in its fifth week of release.

And debuting at No. 111 was *Home Room*, with a weekend gross of $3,467.

By the end of the week, the total gross was at $5,216, meaning that about 620 people had seen it—and that was the end of the theatrical road for *Home Room*. Just one month later, it was released on VHS and DVD. Now you can buy a copy for $20 or less, or rent it for the cost of a large popcorn at the movies.

Ours is not a perfect movie world. Virtually every weekend, we get another crappy, big-budget action movie filled with explosions and car chases and stupid dialogue, or another romantic comedy with limp banter and a hug-at-the-airport ending—and millions will attend these movies. So many of these films are populated by good-looking stiffs, or cheesy actors hamming it up like clueless soap opera stars. Yet only a few thousand adventurous types have ever seen Busy Phillips' astonishing work in the well-crafted and honorable *Home Room*.

Such a shame.

The brilliantly funny Denis Leary and the brilliantly photogenic Elizabeth Hurley must have some friendship if
they're still talking to each other these days, seeing as how
Leary and Hurley have headlined two movies together—
and neither one was ever given a theatrical release. Imagine spending all that time together with nothing to show
for it!

And that's the real heartbreak of the Lost Movie.
Even if a film is lousy—and neither of the Leary/Hurley
collaborations will make you forget about Tracy and Hepburn or even Farley and Spade—you have to feel bad for
the actors, the directors, the writers, the producers and
the crew members who labor for months or even years on
a project, and never get the opportunity to present the
movie in a theater to a paying audience. Even if you've
been paid handsomely for your services, you have to feel
cheated when you find out your work is being shelved or
will get a quiet, late-night "premiere" on a cable channel
before being downsized and shrink-wrapped for video
stores.

With that in mind, I went on a scavenger hunt for
Double Whammy and *Dawg*, aka *Bad Boy*, the two films
starring Denis Leary and Elizabeth Hurley, and I pursued
copies of *Ordinary Decent Criminal* and *D-Tox* and *Elephant Juice* and *All I Want* and a number of other Lost
Movies from recent years. Many are available on video; a
few popped up on cable, and I captured them via Tivo. A
couple could be found only on eBay. Some remain MIA.
They never played in theaters, and they've never even
been given an afterlife on home video. They're truly lost.

Here's the lineup from my Unreleased Film Festival, with asterisks next to the ones I'd recommend.

*Ripley's Game

(European release in 2003; American video release in 2004)—The novelist Patricia Highsmith's famously reptilian con artist/killer character of Tom Ripley has been played by four actors: Alain Delon in *Plein Soleil*, René Clément's 1960 version of *The Talented Mr. Ripley*; Dennis Hopper in Wim Wenders' 1977 adaptation of *Ripley's Game*; Matt Damon (in a brilliantly creepy performance opposite Jude Law and Gwyneth Paltrow) in Anthony Minghella's *The Talented Mr. Ripley* in 1999—and John Malkovich in Liliana Cavani's version of *Ripley's Game*. It played in Europe in 2003 but made its American debut on the Independent Film Channel with absolutely no fanfare. Unlike the callow Ripley of the 1999 film who becomes a killer only when he's exposed as a social-climbing imposter, Malkovich's Ripley is older, more polished and sophisticated, and quite comfortable in the knowledge that he "has no conscience," as he freely admits. In *Ripley's Game*, our man is a droll aesthete living in a grand Palladian palazzo outside Venice with his exotic wife, a beloved harpsichord virtuoso. But Ripley has built his life on schemes and cons, and when he's shoved into a corner and forced to return to his wicked ways by a brutish cohort (the great Ray Winstone), Ripley's latest game is to manipulate a dying neighbor into becoming a hit man. Cavani's film is lush and chilling, and Malkovich is almost too perfectly cast as the charming, fiendish Ripley. As of this writing, *Ripley's Game* is still not available on DVD or VHS in the United States; it just showed up on the Independent Film Channel in 2003, and not even the IFC was interested in promoting it. They refused to provide me with a screener copy, and couldn't have cared less if *Ebert & Roeper* featured *Ripley's Game* on our show. I guess that's because the Independent Film Channel has all the viewers it could ever want! In March 2004, we reviewed and recommended *Ripley's Game* as a Video Pick.

Daddy and Them

(Filmed in 1998; released on video in 2004)—Writer/director/star Billy Bob Thornton followed *Sling Blade* with the trailer-trash ensemble comedy *Daddy and Them*, with Thornton and then-girlfriend Laura Dern as a squabbling married couple; Kelly Preston as Dern's randy sister, who once had a fling with Thornton and still has a thing for him; Andy Griffith as Thornton's dad; the late Jim Varney as Thornton's uncle, who's on trial for attempted murder; and Ben Affleck and Jamie Lee Curtis as husband-and-wife defense attorneys who loathe each other. After a disastrous test release in Macon, Georgia, in October 2001, *Daddy and Them* was swept under the Miramax carpet—and now that it's finally out on video, it's easy to understand why. This is a loud, crude, thuddingly unfunny and thoroughly annoying screech-fest, with the actors all shouting and ranting at each other, as if increased volume will somehow make up for the fact that the screenplay is below sitcom level. It's amazing that so many talented people could have gotten together and created such junk.

*Highway

(Released on video in 2002)—A stylish and self-conscious road movie set in the 1990s grunge era, with Jared Leto and Jake Gyllenhaal as petty criminals who incur the wrath of a Vegas mobster and flee for Seattle in pursuit of Gyllenhaal's dream girl from high school. Along the way they hook up with a mind-fried drug dealer (John C. McGinley in a performance so over-the-top it'll leave you giddy) and a remarkably cute and sweet young hooker (Selma Blair), who has left the brothel for the world of freelance hitchhiking. Director James Cox (*Wonderland*) goes wild with the artsy heist scenes and the fancy flashbacks and he ladles on the homoeroticism so thickly that Pat Robertson could spot it. But *Highway* is an interesting journey with a frantic finale set against the backdrop of a Grunge Nation in mourning over the death of Kurt Kobain. It may be a failure, but it's a lot more interesting and ambitious than most theatrical releases that fall short.

Dawg

(Released on video in 2002)—This one was doomed from the start by a deadly screenplay, with Denis Leary as a womanizer with almost magical powers to seduce all manner of women. Elizabeth Hurley plays the beautiful attorney who informs him that his deceased grandmother has left him $1 million—but he can collect only if he can track down twelve of his ex-girlfriends and get them to say, "I forgive you." Yeah, that's what Grandma would do. Hurley and Leary drive up and down the California coast as he visits a series of flakes, damaged women and nutcases, all of whom are conveniently available for confrontational scenery-chewing when he stops by. In one particularly grotesque scene, Leary discovers that one of his exes is now a man—and the guy insists on modeling his new physique in raw detail. Hurley looks great and the fast-talking Leary has a few choice moments—but *Dawg* lives down to its title. It's a real barker.

Breaking Up

(Released in two theaters in 1997, achieved a total gross of $4,493; released on video in 1998)—Russell Crowe is in full nerd mode as a photographer who wears giant glasses and bad shirts and has a George Will haircut and a wispy goatee. Salma Hayek is his on-again, off-again, French-teacher girlfriend. We know we're in trouble right from the start as the two appear in split screen, addressing the camera as they recap their tumultuous relationship. "As the relationship has deteriorated, we f— like monkeys," says Hayek. With its black-and-white flashback scenes and its ambiguous ending, *Breaking Up* aspires to be more than just another relationship movie. Those aspirations are not realized.

The Third Wheel

(Scheduled release in 1998 didn't happen; released on video in 2004)—Ten minutes into the movie, I understood why Harvey Weinstein kept this film from theaters for all those years, despite the potential box office appeal of Denise Richards and Luke Wilson as the romantic leads, Ben Affleck in a major supporting role and Matt Damon in a splashy cameo. The problem is a guy named Jay Lacopo, who came up with the made-for-TV plot about shy guy Wilson finally getting up the nerve to ask bombshell co-worker Richards for a date—prompting everyone else in the office to create a betting pool on whether he'll hold her hand, kiss her, etc., etc., on their first night out. Even worse than the script is Lacopo's mannered and amateurish performance as the title character, a mysterious homeless man who plunks himself into the middle of the date and ruins everything—or does he? By the time I got to the closing credits, with Lacopo breaking character and leading the supporting cast in an extended parking lot dance sequence as he lip synchs to "Bust a Move," I was holding my head in anguish. What is this guy doing! It's a shame too, because Wilson and Richards have a sweet and easy chemistry, and Affleck is funny as the loutish but loyal sidekick. He's the kind of guy who shows up for the office Halloween party in a cheap suit with a padded gut and a baldy cap and says, "I'm your dad."

*Killing Me Softly

(Originally scheduled for a 2002 theatrical release; released on video in 2003)—Heather Graham alert! Get the unrated home video version of this otherwise unremarkable, third-rate Hitchcock imitation about a naïve American girl in London who falls into a steamy and dangerous love affair with a handsome adventurer (Joseph Fiennes from *Shakespeare in Love*). Ms. Graham participates in some of the most explicit love scenes performed by a mainstream actress since Halle Berry in *Monster's Ball*. After an intriguing setup and a couple of hot love scenes, *Killing Me Softly* turns into a ludicrous thriller with a howler of a "twist." Still, I'm recommending it for camp value and for the Heather Graham factor.

Too Smooth
(Filmed in 1998; released on video in 2002)—Neve Campbell and Rebecca Gayheart are front and center on the video cover, but they have supporting roles. The real stars of *Too Smooth* are the two unknowns in the background: the cute but wooden Katie Wright, and the Patrick Dempsey-ish Dean Paras, who also wrote and directed this harmless but tired romantic comedy about a truth-bending womanizer who must make amends before he can find true love. (Where have we heard that before?) Campbell and her brother Christian Campbell, who also appears in the film, are listed as producers. Campbell plays Paras' former high school girlfriend, a fragile nutball actress who's still in love with him. Gayheart is the goodtime-girl waitress who immediately wants to bed him. Amazing how well these guys do with the ladies when they write and direct parts for themselves!

Ordinary Decent Criminal
(Filmed in 1999; released on video in 2003)—The creatively audacious, publicity-hungry, cop-taunting Dublin criminal Martin Cahill has been the subject of a BBC-TV movie, John Boorman's *The General* and the more fanciful *Ordinary Decent Criminal*, with Kevin Spacey muffing his Irish accent from time to time in the title role. Still Spacey sounds as authentically Irish as Liam Neeson compared to the actress playing his wife, none other than Linda Fiorentino. Yes, when I think Irish, I think Linda

Fiorentino. Colin Farrell, who has a tiny role as one of Spacey's henchmen, became a star by the time the movie came out on video; hence his appearance on the video box alongside Spacey and Fiorentino. This is another case of deceptive advertising. All told, Farrell has about six lines, and they all include the word "shite." As for the film—it has a few moments and Spacey has loads of charisma, but it's ultimately a misfire.

Elephant Juice

(Released in the UK in 2000; unavailable on video in the U.S.)—An ensemble romantic comedy from Amy Jenkins, creator of the British television series *This Life*. The copy I purchased via eBay wouldn't play on my DVD machines, but it worked fine on my laptop computer. *Elephant Juice* is notable only because it contains the only nude scene in the career of Kimberly Williams, the button-cute star of the *Father of the Bride* movies. Here she plays a chipper, foul-mouthed, sexually charged waitress and single mom, and for a brief moment she's topless in bed. Unfortunately, she and everyone else in the cast are spouting the cliché-riddled dialogue that sinks the film.

When the Party's Over

(Scheduled for a theatrical debut in 1993; released on video in 1999)—Yet another weak ensemble romantic comedy, with Sandra Bullock as a salty free spirit who spouts lines like, "Who the fuck stole my Cap'n Crunch!" and, "Fuck 'em once and they want to put a goddam leash around your neck." Her roommates include the sexually voracious Rae Dawn Chong, and a mousy social worker played by Eliza-

beth Berridge. We also get a painful supporting perfor-
mance from Fisher Stevens as a New Age actor named
Midnight whose verbal repertoire includes such gems as
"We met in another life" and "Death is just a part of life."

WHEN REAL LIFE OVERTAKES REEL LIFE

Sometimes real-world events intrude on the movie uni-
verse, making it virtually impossible to release a film without coming across as insensitive. *Prozac Nation*, based on
Elizabeth Wurtzel's best-selling memoir, was filmed in
2000, with Christina Ricci starring as Wurtzel (we know
from the opening scene that she's deeply depressed because
she's sitting topless on her bed, just staring into space). Jason
Biggs plays her boyfriend, Jessica Lange is her mother—and
in a particularly ironic bit of casting, Anne "Call Me Crazy"
Heche plays her psychiatrist. I saw this well acted but me-
andering and unsympathetic work at the Toronto Film Festival in September 2001, just days before the attacks on the
World Trade Center and the Pentagon. A few months later,
Wurtzel was promoting her latest self-pitying book when
she told a reporter for the *Toronto Globe & Mail* that when
her mother phoned to tell her about the attacks, her first reaction was, "What a pain in the ass." Wurtzel, who was in
New York at the time but slept through the morning, added
that she "had not the slightest emotional reaction . . . I just

felt like, everyone was overreacting. People were going on about it. That part really annoyed me."

This was hardly the kind of publicity Miramax was seeking for an already tough-to-promote project about Wurtzel's self-absorbed little life. The release date for *Prozac Nation* was pushed back. And pushed back again. And pushed back again. Now the plans are for a straight-to-video release.

Here are some other films that were canceled, postponed, pulled from theaters or removed from television and video because of real-world events.

The Manchurian Candidate (1962)

John Frankenheimer's classic about an American soldier who's brainwashed to become an assassin was kept out of circulation for twenty-five years. Urban legend has it that after the Kennedy assassination, Frank Sinatra was so overcome with grief and remorse that he purchased the rights to the film just so he could shelve it. More plausible is the theory that Sinatra got into a profits dispute with the studio and bought the rights just to spite everybody.

A Clockwork Orange (1971)

Director Stanley Kubrick was so horrified after his violent film inspired a series of copycat crimes in Great Britain that he pulled the movie from circulation for years.

SpaceCamp (1986)

This harmless adventure about a group of teenagers who attend a NASA camp and are accidentally launched into space was about to hit theaters when the *Challenger* space shuttle exploded. *SpaceCamp* was finally released several months later, but did little business.

O (2001)

Tim Blake Nelson's basketball-themed update of *Othello* starred the solid Mekhi Phifer and the brilliant Julia Stiles as young lovers, a surprisingly effective Josh Hartnett as the jealous, manipulative third wheel and Martin Sheen as Hartnett's father and coach—and, like Shakespeare's tragedy, it ends with shocking violence. After the April 1999 shootings at Columbine High School, Miramax delayed the film for more than a year.

Teaching Mrs. Tingle (1999)

Also delayed because of the Columbine shootings. Originally titled *Killing Mrs. Tingle*, Kevin Williamson's dark satire featured Katie Holmes as a revenge-minded student and Helen Mirren as the cruel teacher who's keeping her from becoming valedictorian.

Nosebleed (never completed)

This action comedy with Jackie Chan as a window washer at the World Trade Center was in production when the attacks of 9/11 occurred. For obvious reasons, the film was canceled.

Trapped (2002)

In a summer filled with high-profile child-abduction stories, Columbia backed away from this trashy thriller with Kevin Bacon and Courtney Love as kidnappers who steal Charlize Theron's daughter.

Phone Booth (2003)

Joel Schumacher's taut thriller about a New York PR man (Colin Farrell) caught in a sniper's laser beam was postponed due to the Beltway sniper shootings.

Here are some movies that were delayed due to unforeseen connotations to 9/11.

Bad Company (2002)

This god-awful buddy pic starring Anthony Hopkins and Chris Rock was pushed back from December 2001 to June 2002 because of a plot involving a terrorist planting a bomb in New York City's Grand Central Station.

Buffalo Soldiers (2003)

An excellent and widely misunderstood black comedy starring Joaquin Phoenix as a drug-dealing con artist–soldier in West Germany in 1989, this has to be the most frequently postponed movie in modern history. Miramax changed the release date on *Buffalo Soldiers* at least five times—first because of 9/11, and later due to the war with Iraq. Completed in June 2001, *Buffalo Soldiers* was finally released in the summer of 2003 but grossed only $354,000.

Collateral Damage (2002)

On a visit to New York just days after the attacks of 9/11, I noticed a soot-covered billboard for *Collateral Damage*, starring Arnold Schwarzenegger as a Los Angeles firefighter who loses his family when a terrorist blows up a high-rise. If you saw something like that in a movie, you'd say it was too obvious. The film itself, a passable thriller, had been scheduled to open in October 2001, but was delayed for several months.

Sidewalks of New York (2001)

This Woody Allen–esque romantic comedy from Edward Burns was pushed back a few months for two reasons: Paramount felt audiences wouldn't be in the mood for a relationship-centered film about unfaithful yuppies set in Manhattan, and the World Trade Center was visible in several background shots.

Big Trouble (2002)

This frantically unfunny comedy based on a Dave Barry novel was delayed because of a storyline about a nuclear device hidden on a commercial flight.

There's a tendency to think of straight-to-video and straight-to-cable films as modern-day B-movies—but the original B-movies were designed to play prior to the main feature with the big stars, and they usually starred second- or third-tier actors. Today's Lost Movies often feature some pretty big names still in their prime or just a few years removed from their biggest hits. A partial list of actors with at least one Lost Movie on their resumes, and the year the movie was released on video in the United States:

Woody Allen: *Picking up the Pieces* (2002)

Alec Baldwin: *Thick as Thieves* (2001)

Kathy Bates: *Unconditional Love* (2003)

Mischa Barton: *Tart* (2000)

Pierce Brosnan: *Grey Owl* (2001)

Sandra Bullock: *Fire on the Amazon* (2000)

Michael Caine: *Shiner* (2002)

Russell Crowe: *Breaking Up* (played in two theaters and grossed $12,000 in 1997; on video in 1998)

Leonardo DiCaprio: *Total Eclipse* (played for one week in the United States and grossed $340,000; available on video in 1997)

Robert Downey Jr.: *Hugo Pool* (theatrical release in 1997 didn't happen; on video in 1998)

Minnie Driver: *Slow Burn* (2000)

Will Ferrell: *The Suburbans* (2000)

James Gandolfini: *Dance With the Devil* (2003)

Anthony Hopkins: *The Devil and Daniel Webster* (2001 release was scrapped; still not available on video)

Holly Hunter: *Woman Wanted* (2000 release didn't happen; not available on video)

Kate Hudson: *Ricochet River* (2001)

Diane Lane: *The Only Thrill* (1999)

Frances McDormand: *Talk of Angels* (2004)

Mike Myers: *Pete's Meteor* (2003)

Nick Nolte: *The Best of Enemies* (planned for a 1999 release but never made it to theaters; not available on video)

Haley Joel Osment: *Edges of the Lord* (2001 release
    was scrapped; still not available on video)

Al Pacino: *Chinese Coffee* (2000 release never
    happened; still not available on video); *Two Bits*
    (released in 1995, grossed $26,000; released on
    video in 1997)

Brad Pitt: *The Dark Side of the Sun* (theatrical release
    in 1997 didn't happen; not available on video)

Marisa Tomei: *Just a Kiss* (grossed $64,000 in
    theaters in 2002; on video in 2003)

Robin Williams: *The Secret Agent* (1996)

Luke Wilson: *The Third Wheel* (2004)

Elijah Wood: *All I Want* (2003)

Epilogue: In America

"If you love movies so much, why did you write a book making fun of movies and movie stars?"
—Question I heard about a thousand times after my last book, *10 Sure Signs a Movie Character Is Doomed & Other Surprising Movie Lists*.

Chicago, November 2003. On a bone-chilling Saturday morning, coffee in hand, I arrive at a multiplex on the city's North Side to see an upcoming film titled *In America*. This screening has been set up for me after a last-minute scheduling snafu kept me from attending the regular press screening, and as I search for a seat, I do a quick head count. There are fourteen other people in the room, and I have no idea who they are or how they came to be here.

After a twenty-minute delay due to technical problems,

the lights finally dim. I try to forget about the hard seat and the teeth-chattering chill in the theater as the movie begins.

One hundred and three minutes later, the closing credits begin to roll. As if waking from a dream, I'm suddenly reminded that I'm still wearing my coat and I'm still holding the cup of coffee I'd been nursing, and the theater is still cold and the seat is still uncomfortable. There are other people in this room, and there's a whole Saturday world outside, with people doing chores around the house, running errands, having lunch, going to the movies. None of that registered as I watched *In America*.

Jim Sheridan's semiautobiographical masterpiece tells the story of an Irish family that comes to New York to start a new life after the tragic death of the youngest boy, Frankie. The story follows Johnny (Paddy Considine) and Sarah (Samantha Morton) and their daughters, eleven-year-old Christy and six-year-old Ariel, played by real-life sisters Sarah and Emma Bolger.

They have no money. They live in a junkie-infested building in Hell's Kitchen. The downstairs neighbor seems to be dangerous and insane. The girls are shunned at school. And their grief over Frankie's death haunts every waking moment.

It's a bleak scenario, and yet *In America* contains some of the more uplifting and inspirational moments in recent cinema history. We see the story through the eyes and the memories (and sometimes the video camera) of eleven-year-old Christy, an incredibly resilient child who has essentially been raising her six-year-old sister for the past year while her mother and father struggle to cope. As grounded as Christy must be, she's also a little girl who believes in the power of magic wishes, and each time she uses one up, you find yourself aching for those wishes to come true.

This is a shamelessly sentimental story, but not once did I feel manipulated. The emotional highs and lows are authentic and universal. Before the year is out, I will place *In America* atop my Ten Best list, and I will write a column urging people to see it and promising a money-back refund to the first 100 people who find it wanting. (The column generates more than 300 e-mails, phone calls and letters of agreement— and exactly 13 requests for refunds.) Every once in awhile, I see a movie that I know will stay with me for the rest of my life, and my life will feel a little bit richer for the experience.

This is one of those movies.

Some movies are priceless. Others, not so much. Still, whether you're crying with a movie or laughing at it, the filmgoing experience is almost always just about the most fun you can have in a dark room for two hours.

As much as I loved *In America*, I also revel in movies like *Basic Instinct*, with its lurid cinematography, its howlingly awful dialogue and its ridiculous plot about a bisexual authoress serial killer, played by Sharon Stone, whose performance lives down to her last name. A decade after *Basic Instinct* was released to strong protests from gay groups, scathing reviews and big box-office, I clicked across the last few minutes of the film on cable, and I found myself cackling with glee. A deeply tanned Michael Douglas, his jaw clenched, makes out furiously with Sharon Stone as the unbelievably obvious music pounds and pounds and POUNDS TO A CRESCENDO AS THEIR LOVEMAKING REACHES A FEVERED PITCH . . .

And then they talk about the future. "We'll f—— like minks, have lots of rug rats and live happily ever after," says Douglas. "I hate rug rats," replies Stone. "Okay," says Douglas. "We'll f—— like minks, forget the rug rats and live happily ever after."

They start to make love again, and the MUSIC BUILDS AGAIN, LOUDER AND FASTER, LOUDER-FASTER-LOUDER, and the camera pans under the bed, and we see the damning piece of evidence identifying the real killer!

My God, it's terrible. And also quite wonderful.

If I hear a horrible song on the radio, I leap for the dial. If I come across a rerun of a sitcom I hated, I quickly change the channel. Hell, if I see somebody I'd rather avoid, I'll cross the street or turn the corner as quickly as possible.

But a bad movie—a seriously bad movie, like *Basic Instinct*—is something to embrace.

It has Schlock Value.